OPENED
FROM THE
INSIDE

Taking the Stronghold of Zion

BOB SORGE

Oasis House
Kansas City, Missouri

Other books by Bob Sorge:

• *IT'S NOT BUSINESS, IT'S PERSONAL*
•*POWER OF THE BLOOD: Approaching God With Confidence*
•*UNRELENTING PRAYER*
•*LOYALTY: The Reach Of The Noble Heart*
•*FOLLOWING THE RIVER: A Vision For Corporate Worship*
•*ENVY: The Enemy Within*
•*SECRETS OF THE SECRET PLACE*
•*Secrets Of The Secret Place COMPANION STUDY GUIDE*
•*Secrets of the Secret Place LEADER'S MANUAL*
•*GLORY: When Heaven Invades Earth*
•*DEALING WITH THE REJECTION AND PRAISE OF MAN*
•*PAIN, PERPLEXITY, AND PROMOTION: A Prophetic Interpretation of the Book of Job*
•*THE FIRE OF GOD'S LOVE*
•*THE FIRE OF DELAYED ANSWERS*
•*IN HIS FACE: A prophetic Call to Renewed Focus*
•*EXPLORING WORSHIP: A Practical Guide to Praise and Worship*
•*Exploring Worship WORKBOOK & DISCUSSION GUIDE*

OPENED FROM THE INSIDE: Taking the Stronghold of Zion
Copyright © 2010 by Bob Sorge
Published by Oasis House
PO Box 522
Grandview, MO 64030-0522

www.oasishouse.com

Edited by Katie Hebbert and Edie Mourey

Printed in the United States of America
ISBN: 978-0-9826018-2-2
Library of Congress Control Number: 2010939060

Thanks

To Ed Hackett, Gary Wiens, and Aaron Walsh, thank you for your encouragement to write this book. It was your enthusiasm for this message that spurred me to put it into writing.

To Edie Mourey and my daughter, Katie Hebbert, thanks for your editorial help.

To Brian Griffith, thanks for exercising your creative juices to meet the challenge of generating a fitting cover design.

To Dale Jimmo, thanks for the nice touch on the layout.

To my assistants, Marie Grotte and Hollie Carney, thanks for all your labors to help get this message out.

To my wife Marci and my children, Joel, Katie, and Michael, thanks for helping me process rigorous decisions such as titling and cover design.

To my Lord Jesus Christ, thank You for taking on the stronghold of death that we might share in Your life. Your cross gives us courage to take on the strongholds before us. As we partner with You in Your victory, may the fame of our Father's name be glorious in this final hour.

Contents

Introduction

This book centers on a little-known story in the Old Testament—the time when David conquered the stronghold of Zion in order to make it his governmental headquarters.

Here is the biblical account of that conquest.

And the king and his men went to Jerusalem against the Jebusites, the inhabitants of the land, who spoke to David, saying, "You shall not come in here; but the blind and the lame will repel you," thinking, "David cannot come in here." Nevertheless David took the stronghold of Zion (that is, the City of David). Now David said on that day, "Whoever climbs up by way of the water shaft and defeats the Jebusites (the lame and the blind, who are hated by David's soul), he shall be chief and captain." Therefore they say, "The blind and the lame shall not come into the house." Then David dwelt in the stronghold, and called it the City of David. And David built all around from the Millo and inward. So David went on and became great, and the LORD God of hosts was with him (2 Samuel 5:6-10).

In the duplicate account of this event in 1 Chronicles, the man who actually climbed the water shaft and became captain of the army is identified.

Now David said, "Whoever attacks the Jebusites first shall be chief and captain." And Joab the son of Zeruiah went up first, and became chief (1 Chronicles 11:6).

In the pages that follow, we are going to trace Joab's steps as he navigated the water shaft and opened up the stronghold of Zion. The biblical text of this incident is extremely brief, leaving us with many questions about how this conquest actually transpired. As an author passionately committed to the integrity of God's word, I am resolved to remain faithful to the biblical text while at the same time imagining (perhaps with some literary license) how some of the events might have happened.

The point of the book is this: Taking the stronghold of Zion is a prophetic picture that helps instruct us as we seek to conquer the strongholds we face in our own lives.

Here is a quick overview of the journey we are about to take.

- We will look at why Jerusalem, more specifically the stronghold of Zion within Jerusalem, was so important to David.

- We will consider how David's mighty men earned their place of honor in the army, and then we will look at the epic event that qualified Joab to serve as their captain.

- In Part One, the stronghold of Zion will be shown to represent obstacles in our lives today that resist the increase of God's kingdom in and through us. Primarily, we will examine Zion as representing the stronghold of physical infirmity that exists in the church today.

- The emphasis of Part Two will be to equip us with practical ways to engage the strongholds before us. True, we will face dark uncertainties; but through the power of the Holy Spirit and faith, we have been given everything we need in Christ to overcome in this life. Second Peter 1:3 says it this way, "…as His divine power has given to us all things that pertain to life and godliness, through the knowledge of Him who called us by glory and virtue."

My purpose in writing about the stronghold of Zion is to paint a word picture. I want you to be able to visualize what the stronghold might have looked like and to picture in your mind's eye how taking the stronghold may have happened. Once you are able to visualize the actual scene, you will find yourself in the story and will see how the challenge before you is like that stronghold. As you follow Joab's path in penetrating the stronghold, the Holy Spirit will show you ways you can advance against the stronghold you face.

Do you face a daunting spiritual challenge? Do you feel that you have come under attack in specific ways by demonic forces? Is there a wrong way of thinking in your life or family that has become so entrenched that it is now a stronghold? Do you face a seemingly unconquerable illness or infirmity? Are you staring at an overwhelming financial wall? Is there an important relationship in your life that is stressed and strained, and no amount of effort on your part can seem to bring healing? If you are facing a stronghold in one of these areas, then this book is for you.

Maybe you are already aware that the challenge you face is supported by demonic energy that is resisting change. The enemy is squatting in a place where he does not belong, and he has barricaded himself in. He has no intention of ever relinquishing this ground. For your part, you desire to take on this spiritual challenge and see the powers of darkness evicted from your life and the lives of your family and friends. As you engage in this warfare, the taking of the stronghold of Zion will appear before you like a living parable. The story will serve as a picturesque tutorial showing you how to engage the challenges you face. Once you see it, you'll know how to attack it!

My prayer is that the Lord will use this book to give you insight into the taking of your stronghold, and that the power of God will be present to strengthen you until your mountain comes down and the kingdom of God is established fully in your life.

Let us begin, then, by coming to the place that is center stage in the drama before us, the city of Jerusalem.

Part One

The Taking of Zion

1

Goliath's Talking Head

> And David took the head of the Philistine
> and brought it to Jerusalem, but he put his
> armor in his tent (1 Samuel 17:54).

"Give me that head!" David snapped.

Joniah stared back. "You want this thing?" he asked, holding up Goliath's skull by its hair. Joniah was on cleanup duty after the defeat of the Philistines, and he was intending to throw Goliath's head into a burial pit. He couldn't understand why David would have any use for something so big, so ugly, and so dead.

"Yes. Give it to me," David repeated. "You can dispose of the body, but I want the head."

"If you don't mind my asking, what are you planning on doing with it?"

"Too much to explain. Just give it to me."

With a shrug, Joniah handed Goliath's skull over to David. "Whatever. You killed him. It's yours."

As he laid hold of Goliath's hair, the dead weight of the thing caught David off-guard. Bracing his arm, David looked at the vacant eyes and muttered under his breath, "I'm taking you to Jerusalem."

Jerusalem! After defeating the Philistines, Saul would have led his troops back to Gibeah, Israel's capital city at the time. Instead of going *through* Jerusalem, however, Saul would have led his troops *around* it. Circumventing Jerusalem made the trip easier by avoiding its rigorous climb.

Protocol might have bid David to stay at King Saul's side all the way to the royal headquarters in Gibeah. David, however, was compelled by another errand. He had some business of his own to attend to in Jerusalem.

That would explain why David, just as the other troops were taking the more level path for Gibeah, quietly broke rank. Slipping away from the troops and turning to the east, David took Goliath's skull in the crook of his arm and ascended the pass leading up to Jerusalem. "Don't worry about me," he called to a group of warriors who had quizzical looks on their faces. "I won't be long. I'll meet up with you in Gibeah."

Why Jerusalem?

The biblical narrative tells us that, "David took the head of the Philistine and brought it to Jerusalem, but he put his armor in his tent" (1 Samuel 17:54).

You can't help but wonder: Why did David take Goliath's head to Jerusalem? At first glance it appears random and perplexing. Jerusalem is not mentioned once during Saul's reign. In fact, other than this solitary reference, it is mentioned nowhere else in the first book of Samuel. The town had no significant role whatsoever during that time. Saul is never mentioned as ever speaking of or visiting the place. In Saul's day, it was almost as if Jerusalem did not even exist.

But Jerusalem had David's attention. Why?

The most reasonable answer seems to lie with the prophet Samuel. We know from 1 Chronicles 9:22 that long before David was king, Samuel had briefed him privately on some of God's purposes for the kingdom of Israel and the worship of the temple. It is possible that Samuel quietly told David about the significance of Jerusalem as early as the time when he anointed David king over Israel (see 1 Samuel 16:13). But this is only conjecture.

We can only guess as to when and how David learned about the importance of Jerusalem in God's plan. Was it Samuel? Did God tell David directly? Either way, we know this much: By the time David killed Goliath, he already had divine information on the prophetic significance of Zion. He had learned that, once he was king, he was to establish Jerusalem as his headquarters and set his throne on the hill of Zion. Psalm 132:6-14 seems to indicate that David knew this while still a shepherd in Ephrathah, which was Bethlehem, the town where he grew up.

Jerusalem was going to be the capital city of Israel. *That's* why he took Goliath's head there.

What Made Zion a Stronghold?

But there's more to the story. At the time, Jerusalem was a city with two boroughs or communities. The larger section of town was inhabited primarily by Israelites from the tribe of Benjamin. The second section of the city was called Zion. Zion's size was actually quite small, a suburb of sorts, nothing more than a sequestered neighborhood.

The thing making Zion unique was that it was fortified by its own large, protective walls. It was a fort or citadel within the city. In the vernacular of the day, it was called a "stronghold" (2 Samuel 5:7) and was inhabited by Jebusites[1]. Jebusites were Gentiles, long-time natives of the land, and they had occupied this stronghold for centuries.

A stronghold, at that time, was defined as a tract of land especially suitable for self-defense against invasion because of the natural topography of the terrain. Thus, Zion was a relatively flat hilltop that was flanked on three sides by steep escarpments. Above the cliffs rose the walls of the fortress.

If an attacker came against Zion from the east, south, or west, he would first have to scramble up a sharp, natural embankment of rock, then scale a tall, perpendicular stone wall. While attempting this kind of feat, the defenders inside the stronghold would shoot arrows, hurl projectiles, pour hot oil, and do whatever else was at their disposal to deter invaders from scaling the walls of the fortress. Thus, it was virtually impossible to penetrate Zion on those three sides.

If an attacker came against Zion's fourth side—the north— he would be stopped by a perpendicular wall and a thick iron gate. And the same barrage of deterrents would bombard him from the top of the wall.

Additionally, if under an extended siege, Zion was equipped to survive because of its built-in water supply. It was located adjacent to the Gihon spring, and water from the

---

1 The Jebusites were so named because Jerusalem's early name was Jebus. The Jebusites were one of many tribes sprinkled throughout the land of Canaan. We could call them Canaanites since they lived in Canaan, but the more precise term would be Jebusites.

spring was channeled through underground passageways to a pool deep inside the fortress. Using a rope and bucket, drinking water for the city was drawn up from the reservoir below. With a constant fresh water supply, the inhabitants of Zion could weather a siege almost indefinitely.

In other words, Zion was impenetrable.

And this was the problem for David. He had a divine mandate to conquer Zion[2], but no one had ever been able to do it.

A History of Successful Defense

The stronghold of Zion had a long history of successfully withstanding invasion. During the taking of Canaan, Joshua and the children of Judah could not drive out the Jebusites from the stronghold (Joshua 15:63; Judges 1:8). Later, when the Benjamites settled in Jerusalem, they too were unable to dislodge the Jebusites from the barricaded stronghold (Judges 1:21). Then when Saul became king, there is no record that he even attempted to evict the Canaanites from Zion.

I wonder what David's initial reaction was when God told him that one day he was to conquer Zion. Was the idea initially intimidating? Or did God's message come with a rush of faith and confidence of victory?

All we know for sure is that at a time when Jerusalem was not even remotely on Saul's radar, a young warrior named David kept a carefully guarded secret. He understood the prophetic significance of an impenetrable stronghold inside Jerusalem called Zion.

What is a Biblical Stronghold?

In its earliest definition, a stronghold was fort-like and easily defended because of the natural lay of the land. But over time the biblical word "stronghold" came to mean more than just a piece of ground. David gave the word spiritual significance when he called God "my stronghold" (Psalm 18:2; see also Nahum 1:7). Paul, in turn, expanded the meaning of the word even further when he used it to describe how demonic

---

2   "For the LORD has chosen Zion; He has desired it for His dwelling place: 'This is My resting place forever; here I will dwell, for I have desired it'" (Psalm 132:13-14).

powers will establish a beachhead of influence in the souls and minds of people.

> *For the weapons of our warfare are not carnal but mighty in God for pulling down* **strongholds**, *casting down arguments and every high thing that exalts itself against the knowledge of God, bringing every thought into captivity to the obedience of Christ (2 Corinthians 10:4-5).*

Demonic powers seek to establish strongholds of wrong thinking and wrong behavior in our lives. A stronghold can develop in an individual's mind by believing the enemy's lies. A stronghold can also develop in the minds of a generation or community if that generation agrees together to believe in a lie. *Stronghold* is fittingly used to describe this kind of demonic activity because the enemy has found a place of protection behind our walls of unbelief. To displace the enemy from this tower of strength can appear formidable indeed.

A spiritual stronghold, therefore, can be said to be *any kind of demonic power or obstacle that seeks to hinder the advance of the kingdom of God in the life of a believer.*

We can learn to overcome spiritual strongholds by studying how David took the stronghold of Zion. Zion stood as a hindrance to the purpose of God for Jerusalem and the nation. Zion had to be conquered so that the headquarters of Israel's government could be placed there.

When David brought Goliath's head to Jerusalem, he was carrying a burden in his soul. The stronghold of Zion remained intact and unchallenged, and it needed to be brought down.

Goliath Stares Down Zion

But what did Goliath's head have to do with Zion? Why did David bring Goliath's head to Jerusalem?

Let me explain. Since the citadel of Zion was inhabited by Jebusites and closed to visitors, he would not have been able to take Goliath's skull into Zion. Instead, he would have taken it to the open part of Jerusalem where the Benjamites resided.

It is reasonable to suppose that David sought out a part of Jerusalem that was in full view of Zion's walls. He found a flat piece of rock, set Goliath's head on top of the rock, and turned the skull to face the fortress of Zion.

With Goliath's empty eyes staring down the stronghold of Zion, I can almost hear David speaking into the air, "One down, one to go." In other words, David was pledging in his heart, "As certainly as Goliath has come down, you too, Zion, are coming down."

Goliath's head became a silent omen speaking impending doom to "impenetrable Zion." The same anointing that caused a stone to fell a giant would one day penetrate an insurmountable stronghold. It would be twenty years before Zion would fall, but a pronouncement of Zion's collapse had now been made through a prophetic act with a dead giant's head.

Zion would surely be taken!

2

David's Mighty Men

Let Your hand be upon the man of Your right hand, upon
the son of man whom You made strong for Yourself
(Psalm 80:17).

After placing Goliath's head in Jerusalem, it was yet another twenty years before David was crowned king of the twelve tribes. That's when Jerusalem came under his jurisdiction. For twenty years, David held an inner resolve to capture Zion, but he could not do so until he was given dominion over the city of Jerusalem.[1]

2 Samuel 5:1-5 records David's coronation over the twelve tribes. And in the very next verse—2 Samuel 5:6—we are told of David's first act as the newly-crowned king of Israel.

And the king and his men went to Jerusalem against the Jebusites, the inhabitants of the land, who spoke to David, saying, "You shall not come in here; but the blind and the lame will repel you," thinking, "David cannot come in here." Nevertheless David took the stronghold of Zion (that *is*, the City of David) (2 Samuel 5:6-7).

First came the coronation over the twelve tribes; then came the conquest of Zion. Taking Zion was the most important agenda item on David's to-do list as king of the entire nation.

---

1   David had a profound understanding of the prophetic significance of Zion and Jerusalem. The reader is strongly encouraged to read the Appendix on page 111 to understand the history and destiny of Zion in the redemptive plan of God. The following pages will be more meaningful to you if you will read the Appendix now before proceeding.

David's Thirty Mighty Men

The central player in conquering Zion was a man named Joab. To appreciate Joab's motivation and role in capturing Zion, however, we need to understand the place David's mighty men had in the army of Israel.

David had a powerful army, but there were a few warriors in the ranks who had distinguished military prowess and a reputation as "mighty men." They were part of the company referred to as "the thirty" (2 Samuel 23:13, 23-24; 1 Chronicles 11:15, 25; 12:4; 27:6). David selected his army's leaders from these chieftains because of their military achievements.

Every warrior wanted to be one of David's mighty men. The criteria, however, had nothing to do with family name, social class, wealth, height, weight, appearance, personality, or intelligence. Rather, these men were selected based upon their exploits in battle.

Five Qualities of David's Mighty Men

David's mighty men had five qualities in common:

1. Natural gifting

All of David's mighty men had a strong measure of natural gifting endowed providentially by God. None of them were anemic, skinny, sickly runts. They had a strength of physical frame that was theirs from birth, given to them graciously by God.

Natural gifting was necessary to become a mighty man; it was not enough by itself, however, to qualify for greatness in the army. David's mighty men were all very intentional, therefore, about developing themselves in four additional ways.

2. Physical fitness

It's a wonderful thing to be gifted with natural strength, but for a warrior to excel in battle he must develop that strength. In other words, he must exercise. Work out. Be buff. Chiseled. Lean. He must stay in top physical condition.

David's mighty men maintained excellent physical condition through rigorous exercise. The strong made themselves even stronger.

Physical fitness alone was not enough, however, to qualify as one of David's mighty men. They needed more.

3. Military training

To become a seasoned warrior required proper training. The soldiers in David's army had to graduate from training camp. We can suppose this to be true because virtually every nation requires their soldiers to graduate from some kind of boot camp.

In training camp, they learned how to brandish a sword, how to utilize protective armor, and how to wield weapons such as a bow, spear, and javelin to defeat an enemy. They practiced on one another. Boot camp was all about practice, practice, practice. They were also schooled in battle strategies. The veterans taught the rookies from their wealth of expertise.

It was important to be gifted, strong, and trained; but those three qualities alone were insufficient in themselves. We see this illustrated in the encounter for which the children of Ephraim were trained, armed, and equipped and yet, when it came time to fight, they "turned back in the day of battle" (Psalm 78:9). Even though they had been properly prepared for warfare, they lacked the courage and conviction at crunch time to step forward and fight. They never actually went to battle.

Those who qualified to be one of David's mighty men, therefore, had a fourth feather in their cap. They had actually been to battle.

4. Battle experience

Once on the battlefield, training and preparation cease to be theoretical. This is where "the rubber meets the road." Battlegrounds reveal whether the training of boot camp was effectual. Implementing the things learned in training suddenly becomes the difference between life and death. It is here, in the fray, that a true warrior is made.

Everybody starts small and works his way up. Your first time out to battle, you do not engage the champion of the enemy's army. No, your first time out you hang back and look around for a lonely, terrified, puny little Philistine to take on. You're just relieved if you can survive your first skirmish. Then, as your experience grows, the significance of your encounters increases.

David's mighty men had battle experience and lots of it. They were rugged, hardened, tempered, and seasoned on the front lines. They had accumulated histories of victorious engagements. They knew their stuff. They were veterans.

To become one of David's mighty men, therefore, required that a warrior possess the four qualities named so far: strength of frame, physical fitness, military training, and battle experience. But experience alone would not prepare them for the kinds of exploits some of David's men accomplished. One of them, for example, killed eight hundred men. I do not care how many battles one has weathered, no amount of battle experience will prepare someone to kill eight hundred men single-handedly. That kind of feat is impossible. It cannot be done—without the fifth ingredient, that is. To manage *that* kind of exploit will require, yea demand, a final ingredient.

5. Anointing

This was the great mark that distinguished David's mighty men from all the other troops. To become one of David's mighty men, the anointing of the Holy Spirit had to be upon a man's life. He had to be anointed in battle.

Why was the anointing so essential? Because it was the anointing of the Holy Spirit that enabled the mighty men to accomplish exploits of uncommon valor and significance. Each of David's mighty men had at least one exploit to his credit that was so gripping and unusual that there was only one way to account for it—the anointing. These knew what it was to be blanketed with a supernatural enablement from God, empowering them to execute exploits which surpassed their human abilities.

Applying these Five Qualities to our Lives

Before going further with David's mighty men, let me pause to say that these five qualities that marked their lives are applicable to ours as well. We can learn from their example. We have a great yearning to become mighty men and women of God in our generation, and rightly so. It is biblical to desire to become mighty in the Holy Spirit. Look how we are exhorted in Scripture.

Finally, my brethren, be strong in the Lord and in the power of His might (Ephesians 6:10).

Strengthened with all might, according to His glorious power, for all patience and longsuffering with joy (Colossians 1:11).

Watch, stand fast in the faith, be brave, be strong (1 Corinthians 16:13).

Not all believers are equally mighty in God. Gabriel told Zacharias that John the Baptist would be mighty in the Holy Spirit (Luke 1:17), and then John testified that Jesus was even mightier than he (Matthew 3:11). The fact that Jesus was "mightier" suggests that I could be mightier in the Spirit than I presently am. I don't know how mighty I could possibly become, but I desire to be as mighty in God as He would destine for me personally. This is why I press toward the upward call of God in Christ (Philippians 3:14).

In our pursuit, therefore, of becoming mighty men and women of God, we can learn from each of these qualities that David's mighty men possessed.

1. David's mighty men had natural giftings.

In the same way that they had natural giftings, the Lord also gives gifts to each of us. Some of His gifts include faith, healings, prophecy, discerning of spirits, helps, administrations, evangelism, teaching, giving, exhortation, leadership, etc. (see 1 Corinthians 12:8-10, 28-30; Romans 12:6-8; Ephesians 4:11-12).

We should recognize and identify the giftings, talents, and strengths God has given us. Our most effective battles will likely be fought in the areas where we are gifted from above. Once we have identified those giftings, then we can cooperate with the Lord's grace to maximize those strengths for His glory.

2. David's mighty men were physically fit.

Applying that observation to our lives, we want to be exercised and fit in our spirits. People work out in order to achieve top physical condition; similarly, we can exercise ourselves in spiritual disciplines in order to keep our spiritual senses alert and ready at all times.

The primary way this is done is through a life of prayer. There is no substitute for developing a strong, intimate prayer life that is centered in extravagant passion for Jesus. Add to it the grace of fasting. Learn how to pray in the Spirit. Establish a rigorous regimen of Bible reading, meditation, and study. Live in the word and the Spirit. Grow in understanding. Keep your spirit sharp and alive.

3. David's mighty men were trained for battle.

In the same way, we need to get trained for spiritual warfare. Each of us is a soldier in the Lord's army, and we are constantly seeking to become increasingly useful to our Commander. We want to learn to swing our sword more effectively, with more strength, in a wider swath, and with more skill.

To be practical about it, how can we become more skillful in the word? Thankfully, God has raised up many ministries today that are like spiritual boot camps—they equip "the saints for the work of ministry" (Ephesians 4:12). Take advantage of every opportunity you can find to get trained up! Take Bible classes online; enroll in a Bible training institute; sign up whenever equipping seminars come to your church or city; read books and watch DVDs that equip and strengthen you. Then look for practical ministry opportunities where you can exercise and practice the principles you learned in class.

By the way, the absolutely best way to learn is to teach others. The process of teaching—from gathering to organization to presentation—is the most effective way to master truth. Said another way, training others is one of the best ways to become trained yourself.

4. David's mighty men had battle experience.

With each battle you fight, you gain the experience that is crucial to becoming one of Jesus' mighty men. Press into the power and promises of God. With each victory you are developing a history in God that will become your testimony for the next generation.

To make this practical, say yes to every opportunity for servanthood that the Lord moves you to accept. Say yes to even the humblest responsibilities. As you are faithful in that which is least, you will be entrusted with more.

Learn how to prepare Bible study lessons that you can teach others. Lead a small group study or a prayer group, and labor to increase your effectiveness in that ministry. If you are a musician or worship leader, step forward into the fray and use your gifting on the front lines. Lay hands on the sick. Get equipped in praying effectively for others. Engage willingly in spiritual warfare.

5. David's mighty men were anointed.

Of the five, this is the big one. The anointing breaks every yoke (Isaiah 10:27) and changes everything. More than anything else, covet the anointing of the Spirit upon your life.

To grow in the anointing of the Holy Spirit, deal violently with any compromise or hindrance that would dull or limit the anointing upon your life. Cultivate and practice the presence of God through worship and prayer. Learn how to work together with God and move with the winds of the Spirit. Discover the ways in which the anointing on your life is most strongly expressed. Expect the anointing on your life to mature and develop as you grow in the love and knowledge of Christ.

I just wanted to show how those five qualities are relevant to us. Now let us return to David's mighty men.

Renowned Exploits

The leaders among David's mighty men used their strength and experience, under the anointing of the Holy Spirit, to accomplish extraordinary exploits. This was important because, in order to qualify for a place of leadership, a warrior had to have at least one remarkable feat to his credit that he achieved in a specific battle.

Let's take a look at the leaders and the feats they accomplished.

Adino the Eznite was the first among David's thirty mighty men because he killed eight hundred men in one battle. That's astonishing!

These are the names of the mighty men whom David had: Josheb-basshebeth the Tachmonite, chief among the captains. He was called Adino the Eznite, because he had killed eight hundred men at one time (2 Samuel 23:8).

Eight hundred men—that's nearly as spectacular as

Samson's feat. On one occasion Samson killed one thousand men using nothing more than a donkey's jawbone as his weapon. Adino was as powerful as Samson minus just a little bit. That is stunning, considering that Samson is famous in the Bible for coming under an unparalleled, supernatural anointing of strength. Under that anointing he accomplished many humanly impossible exploits.

Never again was there anyone like Samson. But Adino the Eznite sure came close! He was not the sort of man you would want to make angry.

Next on the list, after Adino, was a guy name Eleazar (2 Samuel 23:9-10). He, too, was a force to be reckoned with. He would have told his story something like this: "We were in battle formation at Pasdammim, facing the Philistine army, and the Philistines happened to deploy some of their most elite troops in our direction. All the other warriors around me began to retreat in fear. As I stood there, the Philistines started moving toward me. Suddenly, the Spirit of God fell upon me, a holy anger filled my soul, and I lifted my sword and stepped toward them. I started swinging my sword, and Philistines began to fall. I kept swinging, and they kept falling. By the time it was over, there were dead Philistines everywhere and my fingers were wrapped around my sword in such a death grip that they couldn't pry the sword loose from my hand. Once I was done, the others returned and cleaned up the plunder."

Third on the list was Shammah (2 Samuel 23:11-12). He, too, had a story: "It was lentil season. We had worked hard to plant, cultivate, fertilize, weed, water, and nurture the crop throughout the growing season. But now that it was time to harvest the crop, a band of Philistines thought they would raid our hard-earned harvest. As soon as a man spotted the Philistines, he lifted up a cry of alarm. Everyone dropped everything and began running for their lives. I stood there with my sword in my hand, watching the Philistines coming toward me, and I wasn't quite sure what to do. Suddenly, a feeling of supernatural energy came upon me, a holy indignation filled my soul, and something inside me said, 'Over my dead body!' As the Philistines approached I accosted them, one at a time. There was no turning back now. It was either them or me. So I stood there and started killing them—one, two, three, four… They kept coming, and I kept swinging my sword. At the end, a few of their survivors stopped, looked at me, turned around, and high-tailed it for home. It was only then that I looked around and realized that the ground was covered with bodies. Talk about an amazing experience!"

Then there was Abishai, who killed three hundred men (2 Samuel 23:18). There was also a tough guy named Benaiah (2 Samuel 23:20-21), who killed two lion-like heroes of Moab. He also killed a lion in a pit on a snowy day. He was famous for taking on a spectacular Egyptian warrior when he himself did not even have a weapon on himself; he wrested the spear from the Egyptian's hand and killed him with his own spear.

These were the most remarkable of the stories from David's mighty men. Bottom line, they were bad to the bone. They not only were muscular, trained, and experienced; they were anointed. And each one had a story to tell.

Qualifying for Leadership

To qualify for leadership in David's army, a man had to have a story of accomplishing at least one outstanding military feat. This helps us to identify a spiritual principle: Places of leadership in the army of God are granted to those who *qualify* through a significant spiritual exploit or accomplishment.

Moreover, the significance of the exploit determined the level of leadership. The more remarkable or demanding the exploit, the greater the responsibility of leadership that was entrusted to that person. Adino, for example, was mentioned first as a primary leader because he killed eight hundred men. In contrast, Abishai killed only three hundred men, so he didn't make it to the top level; he was in the second tier of leadership responsibility (see 1 Chronicles 11:21).

Additionally, each exploit mentioned, for which the mighty men were commended, was accomplished *singlehandedly*. The reason for that was simple. For a man to receive credit for a certain exploit, it had to be clear that he himself was responsible for that victory and not another. So each of their stories had a common thread that sounded something like this: "Everyone else ran, but I stood there by myself and faced the Philistines." Or, "Nobody else was with me, it was just me and the lion." Or, "I was facing a giant, all by myself, and I knew in that moment that either he or I was going to die." The battle may have been lonely, but afterwards there would be no mistaking who was God's instrument for victory.

This characteristic of *singlehanded exploits* is still relevant in how God raises up great leaders. When God is building your personal history (i.e., crafting your testimony), He will sometimes lead you into a battle in which you find yourself terrifyingly alone. Your heart cries for greater support from your brothers and sisters in the body of Christ, but they are not there when you seemingly need them most. Satan would seek to burden you with feelings of abandonment and bitterness toward the family of God. "Why won't my brethren stand with me right now? Why have they forsaken me in my time of greatest need?" The enemy wants to distract you with complaining or self-pity.

God has a strategic purpose, however, for allowing you to face this battle solitarily. When you emerge victoriously from the fray, it will be clear to everyone that the victory was won because of the grace of God resting on your life. That victory now serves as qualification for places of greater servant leadership in the body of Christ.

David wanted his primary leaders to have an outstanding exploit in their history so that the other men in the army would honor and follow their leadership. But he also had a second reason in mind: They in turn would sit on his war council.

The War Council

It was very important to David who sat on his war council. For a man to serve as a general in the army, he had to know what it was like to function under a supernatural anointing. Why? Because when the Holy Spirit came upon a warrior with a rush of enabling anointing, that anointing brought with it a divine gift of faith, supernatural grace, and strength to accomplish impossible exploits. David wanted men at the table who had experienced that kind of anointing firsthand and were confident in what God can do through a consecrated vessel.

David himself knew what it was like to come under an anointing for battle. The first time it happened to him was when he was tending his father's sheep and a lion attacked the flock (1 Samuel 17:34). When the lion clamped down on one of the lambs, a holy indignation arose inside of David and he said within himself, "Over my dead body will you have my father's lamb!" He felt a holy energy come over him like a blanket. He grabbed his sling and rod and staff, headed directly for the lion, and by the time it was done the lion was dead and the lamb saved.

That same anointing came upon him a second time, when a bear attacked one of the lambs. Using the same means as with the lion, David rose up and killed the bear. The same thing happened a third time with the Philistine champion, Goliath (1 Samuel 17:48-50). When Goliath spewed out his disdain for the God of Israel, a surge of divine indignation came upon David. Running toward the giant with holy boldness, David slew him by slinging an anointed stone into his forehead.

God used the lion, bear, and Goliath to build David's history in Him. Those solitary victories gave David the absolute confidence that impossible odds could be overcome through the power of the Holy Spirit. He wanted men on his war council who had ownership of that same reality through personal experience in the anointing.

Sitting at the table with his war council, I can imagine David bringing bold, visionary proposals to the table. "Hey, guys, I've been thinking and praying about Ammon and I need your perspective. The Ammonites have been sending raiding parties against our territories for years now, and none of our conciliatory efforts have been effective. I'm sensing it may be time to attack Rabbah, the capital city of the Ammonites, and avenge their anger. What do you think?" The last thing David needed, in a moment like that, was generals who would begin to tremble and cower in fear and unbelief.

He did not want to hear one of his generals whining, "Oh, David, I don't know. Rabbah? That's the most heavily guarded city between here and Ophir. Ammon's most elite troops are stationed in Rabbah. Nobody has ever successfully defeated Rabbah. David, why not rather go for Damascus or another easier target?"

David was not interested in seating that kind of fear and intimidation at his war council. He wanted men at the table who knew how God could anoint a warrior for a God-ordained battle.

"Rabbah?" I can imagine Adino responding. "There's no question that Rabbah is one of the greatest challenges we could possibly take on. But I remember the time when the Philistines came against us, and I was left to face them all alone. Suddenly a holy fire took hold of my soul, and I grabbed my sword and stepped into the battle. The power of God laid hold of me, and the Philistines fell before me like straw. I know that kind of anointing. And Shammah, my friend here on my left, knows that same kind of anointing. Put me next to him and I'm in."

David's generals strategized in boldness and faith because of their experience in the anointing. In wisdom, David placed these kinds of men on his war council—men who had confidence in the God who fights our battles for us.

A Name is Missing

There are two portions of Scripture that talk about and list David's mighty men—2 Samuel 23:8-39 and 1 Chronicles 11:10-47. The thirty are listed by name, from Adino to Uriah the Hittite. But there's one name missing from both lists. The omission is strikingly curious. All the "top dogs" are listed among the thirty except for the man who was over them all—their captain.

David was not their captain. He was king and commander of the army. The position of captain went to another man, the man who was next-in-command directly under David. The captain was the primary leader over the entire army and over all the generals. He reported directly to David.[2]

The reason the captain's name is absent is probably because of the unique manner in which his appointment happened. It was a story like none other, in a league all its own.

The man who became captain was Joab (1 Chronicles 11:6). We now turn our attention to look at Joab and the unusual exploit that qualified him to be named captain of the army. It has to do with taking the stronghold of Zion.

---

2   The positional equivalent in the U.S. military would be the Chairman of the Joint Chiefs of Staff who reports directly to the President.

3

The Captain of David's Army

Now David said, "Whoever attacks the Jebusites first shall be chief and captain." And Joab the son of Zeruiah went up first, and became chief (1 Chronicles 11:6)

David's mighty men were an ominous force to be reckoned with! They were "tough as nails," exceptionally gifted and anointed, focused, loyal, and had some of the most remarkable tales of adventure.

With five-star generals in his ranks, David had a huge decision to weigh: Who could he appoint as their captain? Who was capable of leading such outstanding veterans? Who in the nation had enough stature that men like Adino and Shammah and Benaiah would salute him? Honor is given to a position, but respect is given to an achievement. David needed a captain for his army, but it needed to be a man with an achievement under his belt that would command the respect of his most decorated generals.

Simultaneously, David faced another great need. As the newly appointed king over all Israel, his first agenda item was to conquer the stronghold of Zion and establish his throne and home there. But who could lead the charge? He needed someone who could penetrate and overturn the impregnable stronghold of Zion.

Eureka! David's mind lit up with a great idea. He saw a way for both needs to be met in one great challenge. Why not make the taking of Zion a qualifier for the position of captain? I can imagine David jumping to his feet and exclaiming, "I've got it! I know what to do! I will appoint as captain the man who penetrates the fortress of Zion first and triggers its downfall!"

The first one up would be the first one over.

Qualifying for Captain

David, therefore, made taking the stronghold of Zion a *qualifying* feat. In his judgment, the defeat of the Jebusites was an accomplishment so demanding that it would automatically secure the salute of the entire army.

So the announcement rang forth throughout the ranks. "'Whoever climbs up by way of the water shaft and defeats the Jebusites...he shall be chief and captain'" (2 Samuel 5:8). As I noted earlier, the account in 2 Samuel 5 does not name Joab, but the sister passage in Chronicles does: "Now David said, 'Whoever attacks the Jebusites first shall be chief and captain.' And Joab the son of Zeruiah went up first, and became chief" (1 Chronicles 11:6).

The reason this triumph would qualify someone to be captain was because the penetration of Zion would require much more than mere swordsmanship. Swordsmanship, together with a powerful anointing, might be able to kill eight hundred men in a single battle; but swordsmanship alone would never be able to defeat Zion. Taking Zion was a challenge akin to our contemporary triathlon. To win a triathlon, an athlete must excel in swimming, cycling, and running; to take Zion, a warrior would have to excel in tunneling, climbing, and swordsmanship.

To take Zion, therefore, would demand an unusual gift mix. It would require strength, agility, ingenuity, endurance, creative problem-solving, swordsmanship, anointing, an intuitive spirit, ability to hear God, lightning reflexes, courage, etc. That same gift mix would also need to be present in the army's captain.

A captain would need the skill set to lead a wide diversity of personalities, formulate effective military strategies in the face of formidable enemies, and navigate unforeseen variables over unknown terrain. Zion would be the proving ground to reveal the man who had that breadth of capacity.

Joab had to qualify—he had to take Zion—before he could become captain. There is a principle here that applies to us all. Sometimes God takes us through a test, trial, or conflict that He views like a "qualifying meet." Once we overcome and pass that trial successfully, we qualify for the next level of spiritual responsibility. This is why it is so important that you overcome in your present trial. A victory in your current struggle will grant you the spiritual authority to step into the next sphere of influence God has designed for you.

Motivated by Incentive

When David announced that whoever defeats the Jebusites will be chief and captain, a young buck by the name of Joab cocked his ears. For an ambitious twenty-something, the prospect of being captain was very alluring. "Captain? Did the king say captain?"

Joab began to turn the words over in his mind. "Captain Joab." He liked the way it rolled off his tongue. Smooth. Manly. Dignifying. "Captain Joab. I like that. It has a good ring to it." In that moment, Joab decided he was in. He was going to give it his utmost.

In wisdom, David provided a strong incentive so that the right person would be motivated to go for it. God often does the same thing in His army. He motivates us to take on certain challenges in the kingdom by assuring us that He will grant greater authority to those who overcome. With enough incentive, we will do whatever it takes—even if we die trying—to conquer that challenge.

To take the stronghold, Joab needed compelling motivation. The task was too rigorous and risky to be engaged without an appropriate reward. No one had ever successfully penetrated Zion before, and the chances of dying in the process were ominously high.

Joab was about to go where no man had gone before.

He was willing to engage in something this perilous only because he desired the reward strongly enough.

Let me be personal with you for a moment. I am facing a stronghold as I write this. A physical infirmity in my throat suffered years ago has left my voice extremely restricted. God has found a way to motivate me to take on the stronghold. More than anything else, I want to touch the healing hem of Jesus' garment. The reward that motivates me is the joy of being loosed from this prison and gaining the power of Christ to loose other captives. More than anything else, I want spiritual authority over the stronghold of physical infirmity.

I had a desire, even in my youth, to minister the healing power of God to the sick and infirm. But I never pursued mountain-moving faith with such desperation and abandonment until God changed everything and provided me with the incentive. What was my incentive? My own need for divine healing. The whole issue became personal for me.

God has many ways to motivate us. Is there a wall before you that hinders your ability to move forward in the kingdom? Do you find yourself willing to do whatever it takes to surmount the challenge before you? If God has motivated you to press into the kingdom with spiritual violence, consider it a kindness. Be grateful, even if the circumstances that are motivating you are painful.

Don't despise the means God uses to motivate you to seek the fullness of the kingdom.

Was Joab a Good Guy or a Bad Guy?

Let's pause for a moment and talk about Joab's shortcomings. In this book, I am presenting Joab as a pattern we can follow, even though he is somewhat of a controversial character. Some folks would question whether it is okay to think of Joab as a spiritual hero worth emulating. And for good reason.

Joab's history was somewhat checkered, so some people respond to him with reservation. "Wasn't he a bad guy?" They remember how he killed Abner in almost cowardly fashion (2 Samuel 3:27). They remember how he killed Absalom in direct defiance of David's order (2 Samuel 18:14). They remember how he killed Amasa in order to get his job back (2 Samuel 20:10). They remember how, near the end of his life, he transferred his loyalties from David to Adonijah, David's son (1 Kings 1:7).

All those things are true. Joab was a feisty character who had serious flaws. It helped, somewhat, that he was the son of David's sister, Zeruiah (see 1 Chronicles 11:6). As David's nephew, Joab had a familial kind of loyalty to David that served him well for many years. However, bitterness toward David slowly took root in his heart, and eventually his loyalty gave way. After serving David faithfully for many years, alas, he did not end his race well.

By the time the story was done, Joab was removed from his office and was ultimately executed by Solomon for his treasonous conspiracy with Adonijah.

So yes, I'm conceding that those who question the worthiness of Joab are right; Joab's example is not entirely worth emulating. He was a rascal who made some really bad choices, especially as he grew older. However, when he was young, he demonstrated great consecration and obedience to God in going after the stronghold of Zion. That is why he's the hero of our story. It is this aspect of Joab's godly character that we are focused upon in this book.

Now let's go with Joab to Jerusalem as he took on the stronghold.

4

Zion's Mocking Taunts

And the king and his men went to Jerusalem against the
Jebusites, the inhabitants of the land, who spoke to David,
saying, "You shall not come in here; but the blind and the
lame will repel you," thinking, "David cannot come in
here." Nevertheless David took the stronghold of Zion
(that is, the City of David) (2 Samuel 5:6-7).

We have said that Joab took the stronghold of Zion. It would be more accurate to the biblical text, however, to say that *David* took the stronghold. Notice in the text above that the feat is ascribed to David, not Joab.

Interestingly, David got the credit for the exploit, even though Joab did all the grunt work. Why does the Scripture ascribe the victory to David instead of Joab?

I see a couple possible reasons. First, David masterminded the conquest. God had given the idea to David around twenty years earlier, and David had pondered and strategized for this battle all those years. He had prayed himself through to clarity on it. The idea to take Zion, therefore, was David's not Joab's. Joab had no idea Zion was on God's radar until David announced it, so it is only right to ascribe the victory to David.

In the same way, our victories over strongholds will not be ascribed to us but to our Commander, the Lord Jesus Christ. We are incapable of taking strongholds in our own strength. We are utterly dependent upon Jesus to help us from start to finish. When the victory is finally gained, we will have no reservations about boldly declaring, "It was Jesus who conquered this fortress."

Another possible reason the conquest of Zion was ascribed

to David is because when Joab finally opened the gate to the stronghold, David was likely the first warrior to enter the stronghold and engage the enemy. David's custom, especially in the early kingdom years, was to lead his troops forward into battle. There is good reason to suppose that, since this was the first conquest in his unified kingdom, David was physically present at the front of the battle lines and leading the charge.

This speaks of the eagerness with which Christ helps us overcome the strongholds before us. He is ready and waiting to join us in the fray. When the stronghold is finally taken, it is altogether fitting to say, "Jesus took this one."

The Stronghold of the Blind and Lame

When David approached the stronghold, the Jebusites bunkered down inside and began to gloat in their invincibility. They were absolutely convinced that David had no means or ability to overpower their defenses. They were so confident in their sense of security that they began to taunt David. And the king and his men went to Jerusalem against the Jebusites, the inhabitants of the land, who spoke to David, saying, "You shall not come in here; but the blind and the lame will repel you," thinking, "David cannot come in here" (2 Samuel 5:6).

In other words, they were saying to David, "Even if you try to climb our walls and come against us, our walls are so protected that even the blind and the lame in our midst would be able to repel you."

The Jebusites themselves were acknowledging that Zion was a stronghold that held the blind and lame.

Since Zion was the stronghold of the blind and lame, my thesis is that the stronghold of Zion most directly represents the stronghold of infirmity, sickness, and disease that exists in the church today.

There are many other kinds of strongholds besides just infirmity. Your stronghold might be in your soul, finances, career, business, friends, faith, school, family, marriage, self-image, baggage from past hurts, society, the nation, etc. As I apply the message of this passage to infirmity and sickness, just apply the same principles to your particular stronghold. The principles in this book are relevant for every kind of stronghold.

In light of the multiple mentions in the text of the blind and the lame, however, we are viewing Zion primarily as representing the *stronghold of infirmity and affliction that holds people captive today.* The defeat of this stronghold represents the breakthrough of divine healing we are seeking.

The Final Frontier

Zion's fortress was the last holdout the Canaanites inhabited in the occupied territories of Israel. It was the only place where the Canaanites had been able to live, prosper, and reproduce *inside the very borders of Israel.* They had their own little Canaanite village where they had successfully preserved all their heathen customs and traditions as well as the Canaanite bloodline. It was an ungodly stronghold of uncircumcised Gentiles living unchallenged within the very precincts of the city of Jerusalem. Elsewhere, the Canaanites had been subjugated or destroyed. But not here. All of Canaan could be conquered except this stronghold. The Canaanites in Zion were determined to hold onto their little patch of real estate. They would not be moved.

We have a similar situation in the church today. The church of Jesus Christ has made advances and forays in all directions, over many kinds of enemies, but there is one stronghold that sits right in the middle of the church and remains unconquered. I am speaking of sickness, affliction, and infirmity, which persist regardless of our repeated efforts to unseat them.

The stronghold of physical affliction is "the final frontier" in the church today. It is as though the enemy says, "You may be able to conquer anything else, but you can't have this one. Sickness is here to stay."

Sometimes it seems as though the enemy talks to us like this: "You can have your worship ministry; you can have an intercessory team; we'll let you have your prophetic ministry; you can do inner healing; we'll let you have financial wholeness seminars; you can minister restoration to broken families; have your preaching and teaching ministry; have your small groups; we'll let you equip children, teens, and young adults; you can have a Seniors group; you can do marketplace ministry; we'll let you do evangelism; you can have a food bank and clothing center for the poor; you can have your crisis pregnancy center; we'll let you have a Bible school and train up a young generation for ministry; we'll even let you have a webcast and media center. But there's one thing you won't have. You will not have a breakthrough in divine healing."

A Mocking Spirit

The enemy does not simply say, "You shall not come in here." He says it with an edge. His voice comes with the sneering, jeering timbre of a scoffing spirit.

"Joshua couldn't take us," came the taunt toward David from within Zion. "The Benjamites couldn't move us. Saul couldn't oust us. And neither can you, David. Get used to it. We're here to stay."

Peter promised that this same mocking spirit would resurface at the end of the age, scoffing the end-time church that is watching and waiting for the Lord's visitation. "Knowing this first: that scoffers will come in the last days...saying, 'Where is the promise of His coming?'" (2 Peter 3:3-4). This mocking spirit derides today's church for its powerlessness. "You have said that Jesus is going to come to you and demonstrate His presence and power with miracles, signs, wonders, and healings. Well...where is the promise of His coming? Where is He?"

This is the reproach upon the church in this hour. We are fasting, praying, contending, and believing for the "greater works" that Jesus promised we would perform (John 14:12), and yet there are multitudes within the ranks of the believing community still bound with affliction, infirmity, sickness, and disease. The stronghold of infirmity stands, seemingly unmoved, right in the middle of the camp of the saints.

I do not mean to sound unappreciative of the wonderful things God is doing in the earth today. I thank God for His great power and wondrous works. God *is* at work in the church. He *is* healing and delivering. We are deeply grateful for each and every manifestation of His divine power. But healings and miracles are relatively few and far between when compared to the compelling need.

The sneering voice coming from the stronghold of affliction seems to be especially reviling toward the church in the western world. I hear it saying, "You're not going to conquer this stronghold of infirmity. Especially not in America. You're too rich, too soft, too lukewarm, too fat, and too wretched. You've got too many doctors, too many medications, too much health insurance, and too many options. There's too much compromise and unbelief in the western church. If you were in some third-world, impoverished nation, you might have a chance at seeing some notable miracles; but not in America. It's not going to happen. Not here."

Jesus is Going to Take this Stronghold

Jesus has an answer, however, for that mocking spirit. It's precisely where they said it *couldn't* happen that He is going to demonstrate the greatest outpouring of His power and glory. He will do this specifically because they said this was the last place this could happen. This will be to the fame of the name of our Father. We have an announcement for the spirits maintaining the stronghold of infirmity in the church today: Jesus Christ, the Son of David, is going to take this stronghold. He has taken it before and He is going to take it again. You cannot withstand our Champion. Jesus is taking you down!

The ministry of divine healing is going to explode once again in the church. *Especially* in the western world! Because Jesus has a way of choosing "the weak things of the world to put to shame the things which are mighty" (1 Corinthians 1:27).

Dearly beloved, buckle up. I believe we are on the cusp of the greatest release of miracles and healing power in the history of our planet. The Son of David has the stronghold of infirmity in His crosshairs. He has set His timer. There is a moment, very soon now, when Jesus will stand up against this stronghold that sits so arrogantly in the midst of His blood-bought church. In that day, we will see the miracles of Exodus and the miracles of Acts, combined and multiplied, on a global level. The stronghold is going to come down suddenly and mightily.

Jesus is going to give us strategies about penetrating the strongholds we face in the church. All it takes is one word from His mouth. "Faith comes by hearing" (Romans 10:17). When Jesus speaks but one word, mountain-moving faith erupts volcanically within us. We are not scrambling to find faith to overcome the stronghold before us; we are waiting on Jesus to speak the word because we know faith will instantaneously be ours in that moment. When God speaks, faith happens.

Joab did not presume to engage Zion without a commissioning from David. Nor do we presume to engage strongholds in our own understanding. We wait until we receive a proceeding word from the Lord. We wait for Him to signal to us both the timing and the strategy for taking our stronghold. Once He speaks, we move forward with confidence and boldness.

Jesus, speak to the stronghold!

5

The Lame and Blind

Now David said on that day, "Whoever climbs up by way
of the water shaft and defeats the Jebusites (the lame and the
blind, who are hated by David's soul), he shall be chief and
captain." Therefore they say, "The blind and the lame shall
not come into the house" (2 Samuel 5:8).

The precise meaning of the above passage is widely contest-
ed among scholars. Some suppose that the lame and blind
could have been maimed soldiers who were placed on the fortress walls to taunt David and his army, saying, "You will never
be able to take this fortress. Even if you tried, the handicapped
would be able to thwart you." Their taunts incurred the hatred
of David's soul. If that interpretation is accurate, David and his
men may have resolved that, after taking Zion and establishing
David's house there, a blind or lame person would never again
be allowed admittance to Zion.

While that's one way to interpret the literal meaning of the
passage, my emphasis is upon its metaphorical meaning.

The lame and the blind are mentioned three times in the
space of three verses (2 Samuel 5:6-8). With such a strong biblical link between Zion and the infirm, I want us to view Zion as
representing the stronghold of infirmity.

And how fitting a picture, that the cursed specter of disease and incapacitation should be portrayed as a stronghold!
Infirmity truly is a fortress of bars—a prison. Its walls are thick
and high and impregnable to human strength. It holds millions
today in its morbid clutches. The lame and blind huddle inside
this stronghold, shackled by disability, manacled by a power
that never extends to them the promise of release.

Hated by David's Soul

David's attitude toward the blind and lame is intriguing: "'the lame and the blind, who are hated by David's soul.'" I connect viscerally with his hatred because I, too, hate infirmity and affliction.

I never quite had this hatred for infirmity until I found myself a prisoner in its stronghold. I said a little bit about my infirmity back in Chapter Three. In 1992, I underwent a throat surgery that caused irreparable damage to my voice mechanism. A mistake by a sincere doctor left me vocally handicapped. For eighteen years my voice has been very weak and painful to use. So I know something about the torment of infirmity first-hand.

And I hate infirmity.

I hate what it does to people. It snakes its cords around the bodies, souls, and minds of its victims, sucks the life out of their spirits, and drags them into its dungeons of hopelessness, loneliness, grief, and depression. There they sit, languishing in their hovels, staring blankly at their screens, looking for any distraction that might anesthetize their suffering and boredom. They exist, but they do not live.

Hope of a normal life? Vanished. Promise of becoming a meaningful contributor to society? Vaporized. Assurance of rising above the handicap and becoming a better person for it? Rarely. Anticipation that someone will be able to do something to lift them out of their pit? Don't hold your breath.

No, this prison is not a place of confidence and expectation. Rather, it's a place of despair, crushing, humiliation, misery, dejection, sorrow, and grinding futility.

Once Satan gets you in his prison, he never lets go. Isaiah pointed to this when he spoke of the king of Tyre who typified Satan. Isaiah said of him, "'Who did not open the house of his prisoners'" (Isaiah 14:17). Isaiah was affirming that once Satan has you captive in one of his prisons, he will never release you. The only way you will ever get out of this stronghold is if someone has enough spiritual power to stage a jail break.

I know what it's like, in the chains of the stronghold's confinement, to experience a barrage of demonic mental harassment. "You're a casualty. You're finished. It's over. You will never again function in your calling. You really blew it to get yourself in here. What's more, God has forsaken you. He's angry at you and He has removed His favor from you. You don't have the faith to get healed. You may as well get used to it, you're going to be in this pit for the rest of your life."

Satan is a ruthless tormentor of the prisoners.

Have you ever thought of the infirm as prisoners? Visit the psychiatric ward of a hospital sometime, look into the eyes of the patients, and see for yourself. Swing by a children's cancer hospital sometime and look at the pale faces that will not see their next birthday. Spend some time with a deformed child in a wheelchair whose speech is slurred and whose body moves spastically due to cerebral palsy. You will see that infirmity is a prison.

When you behold the plight of the captives, grieve their losses and loathe their chains. Hate infirmity.

Shall Not Come into the House

The last phrase of 2 Samuel 5:8 contains the third mention of the lame and blind and places them in an interesting light: "Therefore they say, 'The blind and the lame shall not come into the house.'"

Next time you are in the house of God, look around. How many wheelchairs do you see? How many lame and blind people are worshiping with you? In proportion to the healthy worshipers in the house, the infirm, sick, and handicapped are grossly under-represented. Their presence is almost non-existent.

They are not in the house.

But do not think they don't exist. Your region is *full* of people who are lame or blind or incapacitated to some degree. Do not think that just because they are not in your church they are not in your community.

They are there. They're just not in your church.

And who can blame them? Why would they come to the house when they already know they are going to leave the meeting in the same condition they came? Sometimes the price tag of going to the house of God is simply not worth the disappointment of leaving unchanged.

Let me explain the price tag. When you are severely incapacitated with sickness, infirmity, or handicap, it can require herculean effort physically and/or emotionally to get yourself to the house of God. For some, it demands hours of labor just to get physically prepared to make the trip. For others, the big challenge is the emotional turbulence that twists the soul when placed in a room full of healthy people.

A demon perches on your shoulder. "What are you doing here? You don't belong. There's no place for you here. You're useless to this church. You're dead weight. You're going to leave this meeting more depressed than when you came. Why did you kill yourself to get here? It would have been so much easier to just stay home. When are you going to wake up to the reality that going to church doesn't work for you anymore?"

My own personal pain in this connection is reflected well by Psalm 42:

> *My soul thirsts for God, for the living God. When shall I come and appear before God? My tears have been my food day and night, while they continually say to me, "Where is your God?" When I remember these things, I pour out my soul within me. For I used to go with the multitude; I went with them to the house of God, with the voice of joy and praise, with a multitude that kept a pilgrim feast (Psalm 42:2-4).*

There was a time when I was the one leading the multitude in praise in the house of God; but when I became a captive to a stronghold of infirmity, all of that stopped. Now, I gather all my emotional strength just to go to the house of praise. On the one hand, I long to be there; on the other hand, I am physically incapable of participating in the singing. Consequently, I have come home from church many times with my soul churning. At times it has taken me hours to recover emotional equilibrium. Often I will push myself to go to the assembly of the saints because I believe in it so strongly. But in terms of soul management, it is actually easier to stay home.

Why do I mention this? To express that I personally understand something about the world of the captives. I empathize in ways I once did not. I can understand why most of them do not come to the house when the saints are gathering. With so many hindrances to overcome, it is simply easier for the captives to stay home. That's why they "shall not come into the house."

Instead of gathering with the saints in the house of prayer, they sit in their caves and try to cope with existing yet another day.

Any Day Now

A day is coming—it is any day now—when Jesus will again take the stronghold of infirmity that sits in the middle of the church, and the sound will be noised abroad, "God is visiting His people."

When the sound goes forth that the captives are being set free by the power of God, your church will not know what to do with all the captives. They will come from all over. They will come with their crutches, their wheelchairs, their walkers, their gurneys, their prosthetics, their canes, their oxygen tanks, their nurses, and their families. They will come in ambulances and airplanes. They will come from near and far, in-state and out-of-state.

Once again, church will look like it should—like it looked when Jesus held church during His ministry—with captives everywhere. Church should be a place where the captives come in droves and return set free by the liberating power of the Lord Jesus Christ.

They may not be coming to the house right now, but just wait. The day is fast approaching when wheelchairs will again line the aisles of our gatherings and the captives will be loosed from their strongholds by the glorious power of the cross. Why? Because our David (Jesus Christ) is again going to take the stronghold of infirmity that mocks the church today.

The lame and blind are waiting for this day.

The Implications of Answered Prayer

One reason taking the stronghold of infirmity can seem so challenging and difficult is because of the enormous implications that follow answered prayer.

- The kingdom of God will be established in authority upon the earth, for there is no disease known to mankind that will stand before the end-time church that carries true kingdom authority.

- The Davidic house of prayer will be established in the kind of glory that God intended. David was not able

to establish his 24/7 house of prayer until the stronghold of Zion was taken; similarly, the house of prayer
for all nations will not enter into its full destiny until
the stronghold of affliction in the church is dislodged.
When this stronghold comes down, houses of prayer
will proliferate exponentially in the nations of the earth
and the power of prayer will be unprecedented.

• The glory and momentum of God's activity will not
be containable in our buildings and church infrastruc-
tures. It will overflow to the stadiums of the earth. The
reproach of powerlessness and irrelevance currently
resting on the church will be lifted before the eyes of
the world.

• The joy of the Lord will strengthen the church. The
Scripture says, "Blessed are the people who know the
joyful sound" (Psalm 89:15). I personally believe "the
joyful sound" mentioned here is primarily referring to
the sound of praise that will erupt in the church when
the stronghold of infirmity is breached and the captives
are loosed by the power of God. In that day no one will
be able to contain or restrain the praise. A joyful sound
will explode from the ranks of the redeemed. "This is
our God! He has visited His people! He is with us! God
is for us—who can be against us?"

• Best of all, the return of Christ will be hastened (2 Peter
3:12). That's because answered prayer accelerates kingdom activity. When the power of God is released in the
last days, it will accelerate human history and hasten
Christ's return.

This final principle is so important it bears repeating: Answered prayer accelerates kingdom activity. Let us look at this
principle in the life of Christ.

Answered Prayer Accelerates the Kingdom

When Jesus released and healed the captives, He accelerated the advance of the kingdom in every way. Salvations
increased; disciples increased; enemies increased; persecution
increased. The release of power accelerated and released forces

that were both positive and negative.

When we understand the accelerating power of miracles, we understand why Jesus so often told those He healed to tell no one about it. Because when they broadcasted His miracles, it fueled the envy of His enemies. When their envy reached its fullness, His enemies crucified Him. By fueling their envy, every miracle took Jesus a step closer to His crucifixion

In the end, Jesus' raising of Lazarus from the dead was the proverbial "straw that broke the camel's back." That miracle essentially got Him crucified. When the Father answered Jesus' prayer and raised Lazarus from the dead, that sealed the envy of the Jewish leaders and crystallized their resolve to crucify Jesus.

Answered prayer accelerates world history. When God answers our cry and releases the lame and blind held in strongholds of infirmity, everything on our planet will accelerate—culminating in the return of Christ. We are contending for answered prayer, therefore, not simply to make our lives happier or more comfortable. Rather, we are longing to hasten the return of our Beloved to this earth. We want Him to come and capture the hearts of Jerusalem (Matthew 23:39) and establish His governmental seat in Zion (Psalm 48:2). When He establishes His house of prayer in Zion (Zechariah 6:12-13), then Jerusalem will finally be the lighthouse to the nations that God intended all along (Isaiah 62:1). We cannot rest until we see the Prince of Peace seated on His throne of glory (Matthew 25:31) in the city of Jerusalem!

6

Navigating Darkness

Now David said on that day, "Whoever climbs up by way
of the water shaft and defeats the Jebusites...he shall be
chief and captain" (2 Samuel 5:8).

"He did not hide deep darkness from me" (Job 23:17).

Zion was a self-contained fortress. Provided that they had
food, its inhabitants could survive invasion simply because they had "indoor plumbing"—a water source that came
up under the stronghold. The most valuable commodity in the
arid climate of Israel was water, and the Jebusites inside Zion
had a ceaseless supply.

The Gihon spring flowed nearby, and underground chan-
nels had been constructed to direct the water to an underground cistern inside Zion. Then, a rope was used to lower a
bucket down the water shaft and into the cistern, where the
bucket was filled with life-giving water and pulled back up to
the surface.

With a constant water supply, Zion's residents were able
to resist lengthy sieges. This explains why it had remained un-
defeated for hundreds of years. The water shaft was central to
their survival.

Through David's military prowess, that which the enemy
relied upon for survival would be the very means of their capture.

David provided the strategy for how the stronghold would
be infiltrated. He told his troops, "The stronghold will be penetrated by climbing up the water shaft."

We do not know, mind you, how David landed upon his

water shaft strategy. Did God tell him through divine revelation? Or was David able to conclude, after years of mulling the dilemma, that the water shaft was the best way to take the stronghold? No matter how he came to that conclusion, David was confident in the wisdom and feasibility of his tactic. He announced it with clarity and boldness. He knew, through the anointing of the Holy Spirit, that this was how the stronghold would be infiltrated.

David's troops needed him to give them the strategy for breaching the stronghold, and we have the same need today. We desperately need the Lord Jesus to give us divine strategy for taking the stronghold of infirmity that we face.

Joab Volunteers

When David announced that the stronghold would be entered through the water shaft, Joab caught a vision for the possibility of the thing. It seemed attainable. Add to that the fact that David would make the victor captain over the entire army and Joab was on board.

I can imagine Joab making an appointment to see his uncle, King David. He wanted to talk to the king about tackling the water shaft. The Scripture does not record their exchange, so the following conversation is how it *might have sounded.*

Joab approached the king, bowing, and paying due reverence. "Your Majesty, if it pleases the king, I would like permission to give it a go. Please let me attempt the water shaft. I am willing to serve as captain of the army."

"Certainly," David replied. "You have as good a chance as anybody. Go for it! The first one up is it."

"Um, your Majesty," Joab paused awkwardly, not sure how to ask the next question. "Mind if I have a look at a map of the city? I would really like to see how the stronghold is laid out."

"We have no map."

"No map?" Joab took a long breath. "Huh. Well...how about a schematic of the tunnel system?"

"We have no schematic."

"No schematic. Hmm." Joab's mind was racing. He had only one more minute with the king, and he needed to get as much information as possible. "Then can you at least tell me which direction the tunnels run?"

"Nobody knows."

"Then how, my lord, am I to access the underground tunnels?"

"Good question, Joab. I'm sorry, but I don't know."

"But if I happen to find my way down the right tunnel, my lord, how will I know when I have arrived at the place where the water shaft leads up into the city?"

David's answer was no different. "I'm sorry, Joab, but we have been unable to get any information whatsoever. That's the problem with this assignment. No one has ever negotiated the tunnel system, so no one can tell us how to do it. But it's the only weak spot in their defenses. The only thing I know for sure is that it's the right way to get in."

David paused. Then he looked straight into Joab's face and continued.

"If you choose to accept this assignment, Joab, prepare yourself to go where no man has gone before. You'll be taking your life in your hands. But if you succeed, I will make you captain. Because anyone who pulls this off will have demonstrated his proficiency to lead the entire army. Are you willing to lay your life down for this cause?"

At first, Joab just stared. Then, with a slow nod, Joab squinted a bit, looked steadily into the king's eyes and said, "I'm in." Once dismissed by the king, he turned around and strode forward without hesitation toward the unknown.

In the Dark

As already mentioned, water was channeled from the Gihon spring via a network of underground aqueducts, and Joab's first challenge was to gain access to that underground tunnel system. How did he get in? We simply have no idea.

One reason we know so very little about how it actually happened is because the biblical record is exceedingly succinct. The Bible gives us literally no details on how Joab pulled this job off. It is left to our curiosity to imagine how he did it.

I have a couple hunches as to how it happened. My first hunch is that this was not a daytime venture. Supposing that Joab had to do some digging to get into the underground tunnel system, I would not expect him to start digging during daylight hours when he could be seen. No doubt he tackled this job under the cover of night, shoveling as quietly as possible so as to avoid detection.

When Joab had dug and finally wormed his way into the tunnel system, not only was it under the black of night, it was also underground. This was before the days of flashlights, and the submergence under water would have made the use of a torch impossible. *There was no light.* The waters were blacker than black. Finally inside the tunnel system, Joab couldn't see a thing. He had no idea what lay before him. He could not see which direction he was facing, nor did he know which way to go.

The darkness Joab experienced was a metaphor for the struggle we will face in tackling the stronghold of infirmity. When we decide to engage this stronghold, we will likely find ourselves navigating corridors of unusual darkness. By saying we will experience "darkness," I do not mean we will succumb to the darkness of sinful temptation; what I mean is, we will find ourselves in a course we have never walked before. We will strain to see into the murky fog before us, and we will likely feel an oppressive spirit as the powers of darkness try to hinder our progress.

Perhaps the darkness you have slammed into is designed by God to prepare you to take on the water shaft.

Sometimes God turns the lights out on us (see Genesis 15:12; Exodus 20:21). He obscures all that is familiar and known, sets our faces on a course that is unknown, and then cuts the lights. When you are first immersed in that kind of darkness, your first impulse is to think that you have sinned. You find yourself asking, "What did I do to bring this on?" The answer, you discover in time, is that the darkness came not because of your disobedience but your obedience. Joseph, for example, found himself in the darkness of an Egyptian prison not because of what he did wrong but what he did right.

This blackness is real. All too real. You cannot see into your future; you cannot see which direction to take; you do not understand why God seems to be so far away from you right now; you cannot see any evidence of God's favor on your life or ministry; you feel the power of the darkness gnawing at your soul and dampening your emotions. It is so dark that you begin to wonder how you even got here.

Darkness, however, is an essential part of the preparatory process for becoming mighty in the Spirit. Here are some of the ways God will use this darkness redemptively in your life.

- He will show you ways in which you have confined God in your thinking. There are elements to the darkness that do not make sense to you theologically. You will be thinking, "The God I know does not do this. But wait. He just did." God will use the darkness to push the ends off your theological box. As I once heard Jack Taylor say, God loves you so much He's willing to look bad for months in order to do you good.

- He will birth within you a new kind of desperation for God. You knew it would be dark, but you had no idea it would be *this* dark. Props you had unwittingly relied upon to keep life working are suddenly pulled away—all of them—and you feel utterly vulnerable. Never before have you felt so desperate for an immediate answer, and never before have you felt so far from finding one.

- The darkness will demand a level of dependence upon God such as you have never had to find before. In the past, you may have known 99% dependence, but this is different. This is 100% dependence. You are so dependent on God it hurts. You need Him for every breath, for every thought, for every step.

- Faith grows at a greater rate, remarkably, in darkness. The darkness challenges your faith to the core. When you fail to understand, you will choose to believe. Endurance is doing its perfect work in you (James 1:4). As you persistently trust, your confidence in God's goodness will become unshakable.

- You will discover sensitivities and abilities in your spirit previously untapped. The rigors of the blackness will summon things from your spirit that you never needed before. You will grow in discernment, understanding, perceptivity, prudence, and in your ability to recognize the voice and will of God. God is enlarging your heart.

- You will come into intimacy with Jesus that is more meaningful and tangible than anything you have known in the past. He is answering your groping by placing Himself within reach so that He can be found (Acts 17:26-27). Later, you will look back at the moment you felt most forsaken of God and realize He was closer than ever (Psalm 91:15). The darkness will birth in you an intimacy so meaningful that you will sustain and guard it carefully all your days.

- You will learn to hear and follow the voice of the Holy Spirit in new ways. Your hearing will become more acute than ever. (When the eyes close off, the ears open up.) You will start to pick up on the subtleties of God's whispers. You will learn to discern the ways of the Holy Spirit. A breath will be as instructive as a shout.

- The intensity of the warfare will exercise your spirit and produce a new strength within you. You will battle your way through oppression, depression, reproach, and perplexity. When you finally emerge from the darkness, you will come forth as a mighty warrior in the army of the Lord.

Perplexity in Warfare

When I was in a season of blackness, one of my prayer concerns was that I did not know how to identify the nature of my warfare. I realized there are four general causative elements in all spiritual warfare—

- God is active in the fray;

- Hell is aggressively involved in the warfare;

- Some things are due to the accident-prone brokenness of the groaning natural realm (Romans 8:19-22);

- Some stuff I bring on myself through my own sin, mistakes, and frailty.

My problem was I couldn't distinguish one from the other in the darkness. I felt like I was taking hits from a sniper, but because I could not see what direction the shots were coming from I felt helpless to defend myself.

It was then that I found strong consolation from Psalm 69:19 where David said, "My adversaries are all before You." David was acknowledging that God had complete insight into the battleground. He knew fully and completely every causative element that contributed to David's warfare.

That Scripture consoled me. Even when I did not know what forces were coming against me, God did. So in the time of darkness, I decided I would not fixate upon my enemy and how he might come against me. Rather, I chose to fix my gaze upon my Beloved. I chose to believe that as I devoted myself to beholding His face, He would defend me and fight the forces against which I felt defenseless.

The Lights Will Come Back On

Lest we make too much of the darkness, I want to end this chapter focused on light. The darkness will not last forever. God will use the blackness in a strategic way to train your soul, but the morning *will* come.

Light is sown for the righteous, and gladness for the upright in heart (Psalm 97:11).

When you enter a season of blackness, the lights go out because the light has actually been sown for you into the ground. To say that light is sown means this: The light you have known has been buried. But because you hold to righteousness, the darkness is never the end of the story. A harvest of light will spring forth.

A day is coming when the darkness will be followed by a new harvest of unprecedented light—revelatory insight into the beauties and glories of Christ Jesus (see 2 Corinthians 4:6).

Additionally, Psalm 97:11 says that gladness is sown for the righteous. Initially that means that your gladness is buried. Joy seems to be extinguished. But joy that has been buried for the upright cannot remain buried forever. It has the seed of divine life in it. That gladness is going to spring up into an abundant harvest of joy. This is the inevitable harvest due the righteous.

Therefore, never relinquish your righteousness! When the lights come on, your joy will know no bounds.

*But the path of the just [the righteous] is like the shining sun,
that shines ever brighter unto the perfect day (Proverbs 4:18).*

7

The Water Shaft

*Now David said on that day, "Whoever climbs up by way
of the water shaft and defeats the Jebusites...he shall be
chief and captain" (2 Samuel 5:8).*

In the last chapter, we left off with Joab in the darkness of the
underground tunnel network. Carefully and methodically,
he fumbled and clawed his way in order to familiarize himself with his surroundings. No matter which direction he went,
there was water everywhere.

We observe, therefore, that by the time Joab was inside the
tunnel system, he was totally and completely *soaking wet.*

Metaphorically, this means that if we hope to conquer the
stronghold that is before us, we must be totally immersed in the
Holy Spirit.[1] This obstacle will come down, not through our resources, talents, or natural strengths, but through our ability to
tap into the power of the Holy Spirit. "'Not by might nor by power, but by My Spirit,' says the LORD of hosts" (Zechariah 4:6).

Perhaps you have been filled with the Spirit in the past, but
previous fillings will not avail in the current crisis. You must be
filled to overflowing *right now,* in the immediacy of this critical moment. You must be soaking wet in the Holy Spirit. Saturated. Baptized. Immersed.

We will talk more in Chapter Ten about the need to be
filled with the Holy Spirit. For now, we are following Joab as
he worked his way through the tunnel network.

Let us trace Joab's steps along a hypothetical timeline.

---

1   In Scripture, water frequently represents the person and work of the
    Holy Spirit. For example, see John 7:37-39.

Crawling Through the Tunnel

1:00 a.m.

Once inside one of the underground tunnels, Joab had to decide which way to proceed. Everything was black, so he couldn't decide based upon what he saw. He had to lean into the anointing on his life and follow the promptings of the Holy Spirit.

He felt along the walls, trying to figure out how the channel was constructed. *It goes in two directions!*

Which way should he go? He had to choose one. And it was critical to his mission that he choose the right direction.

God, help me! Calling upon the Lord, he did his best to discern which direction to take. Finally he made his decision.

For right or for wrong, I'm going this way.

Now he faced another problem. The tunnel was totally submerged. To crawl through it, he would have to take a deep breath, duck down into the water, and then head into it. He did not know if he would encounter any pockets of air as he went, and he did not know how long the tunnel spanned until he would come out to another opening.

This thing could be my grave!

He decided to give it a test run. His plan was to take a big breath, crawl a few feet in, check to see if there might be small pockets of air along the top, and then return back to his opening if necessary.

First he had to set down his sword, digging equipment, and anything on his person that might slow his progress. By the time he had taken all that off, he was stripped nearly naked. Clearly he was taking nothing with him.

One-two-three. Down he went. He pushed himself a few feet into the blackness, then he turned his nose to the top. He tried to breathe in. Water! His nose immediately filled with water.

There are no air pockets, the tunnel is full of water right to the top!

Desperate for oxygen, he clamored back to his opening. *Air!*

He coughed and heaved as he recovered his breath. The channel had been designed to be airtight! Whoever built this passageway had used his head.

Joab sat in the darkness and pondered the implications. Either tackle the tunnel and hazard drowning, or quit and go home. It was all or nothing. *Captain Joab.* That title swirled softly in his dark, wet hole. *Captain. That's me. That's who I am. I was born for this.*

In the loneliness of his silent darkness, Joab made his decision. He was going for it. *If I die trying, at least I reached for something noble in life.*

He prayed one more strong prayer, panted a bit to store up some oxygen, took one final big gulp, and WHOOSH. He was down and in!

Joab wasn't swimming; he wasn't crawling; he wasn't tunneling; he was "scrunneling." He was doing anything and everything to move forward as quickly as he could while using his oxygen as efficiently as possible. He was racing with death itself. He clawed at any rock or crevice where he could get a grip, using it to push himself along. The thought flitted through his mind, *It's too late to go back now. You're committed.*

How long is this tunnel anyways?

He had to stop the thoughts. They were distracting. Every thought had to focus on one thing: moving forward as quickly as possible.

The tunnel kept going. His lungs were bursting. Just when he thought he would pass out, suddenly his hands could no longer feel the top of the tunnel and his head broke the surface.

Air!

Heaving again, Joab took a minute to recover. Then his fingers began to grope around his surroundings. He was in a pool of water, and he found he could almost stand. His shoulders bumped into the walls, and immediately above his head there was no ceiling. It was an opening leading upwards.

Could this be the water shaft? It's got to be!

Under the anointing of the Holy Spirit, Joab had found the water shaft. There was no other explanation—the Holy Spirit helped him find it. This was the same anointing that empowered David to fell Goliath. David had to sling the stone, but the Holy Spirit guided that stone supernaturally to Goliath's forehead. In the same way, Joab had to crawl into the tunnel, but the Holy Spirit guided him to the water shaft. Joab experienced a Davidic anointing.

Climbing the Shaft

1:30 a.m.

I'm not 100% positive this is the water shaft, but whatever it is, I'm going up!

Joab sat and pondered the challenge before him. How would he climb this shaft? He knew it was ludicrous to do so, but still, he had to check—and groping about the stones and bricks, he felt to see if a rope might just happen to be dangling down.

No rope.

Well, of course there's no rope! Joab was actually starting to whisper to himself. *"They're not going to supply you with a rope, Joab!"*

The rope would be lowered only when they were drawing water; otherwise, the rope and bucket would be kept safely on the surface.

Joab realized he was facing the worst case scenario. The only way up was to shimmy. He would have to jam his body up into the opening, and then push upward by getting his fingers and toes wedged into every crack and crevice he could find.

Reaching up, Joab got a finger-hold, and managed to pull his body up into the opening. He leveraged his knees into one side of the shaft and his back into the other side, and then paused to test whether he could hold his position mid-air in the shaft. The stones were cutting into his bare back. Since his body was wet and the stones damp, he had to push extra hard into the stones just to support his weight. Already he was bleeding, and he had hardly started the climb.

No time to lose. Get going.

First one hand went exploring for a nook; then the other hand went looking for something to push up on; then one foot searched for a toehold; then the other knee tried to find a rock it could leverage against. *Push!*

It required all his strength to push on the damp stones, but Joab was now about ten inches higher inside the shaft. And then he did it all over again. First the right hand; then the left hand; then the left foot; then the right knee; then up ten more inches.

That rock is jabbing me in the same place in my back!

Joab knew the cuts in his hands, feet, knees, and back were only going to get worse. But this was not a time to nurse his body or pay attention to his pains. This was a time to push. *Ten more inches!*

Slowly, Joab inched his way in the blackness up the neck of the water shaft.

Good thing I've been working out—this is exhausting!

He ascended the water shaft only through sheer strength. The task called upon every muscle. His life depended upon his muscles to endure this torture chamber.

Eventually Joab wormed his way to the top of the water shaft where he could feel something covering the mouth of the shaft. *The covering feels like wood. I wonder how heavy it is.*

It required all his strength just to support his body in the shaft without falling to his death. How would he ever be able to support his own weight and also push open the heavy lid above his head? He had to find an extra-good grip with both his feet. He groped with his toes until he found the best toehold possible.

Shifting his weight, he found a way to wedge his body in the shaft. He still had to use one arm to hold to the stones, but he was able to free his right arm.

Lifting his right arm above his head, and tightening every muscle in his body, his pushed upward with all his might.

The lid is moving!

Carefully and patiently, Joab worked with the cover until it was moved out of his way. Lifting himself over the mouth of the water shaft, he stepped out onto the surface.

I'm inside the stronghold!

8

Taking the Stronghold

*A wise man scales the city of the mighty, and brings down
the trusted stronghold (Proverbs 21:22).*

2:00 a.m.

Joab paused for a bit to gather his breath, allow his muscles to recover, and to survey the lay of the land. After the darkness of the water shaft, he was surprised how bright the stronghold was under the stars. He was naked and bloody, but no matter, he had a job to do. In a few moments, Joab was on the move.

The Jebusites within the stronghold of Zion were totally unprepared for a warrior to suddenly appear inside their walls at 2:00 a.m.! Furthermore, he was not just *any* warrior. This was Joab, one of the strongest, toughest, sharpest, deadliest men on the planet. Zion was in trouble!

Running quietly and nimbly on his feet, Joab headed directly for the gate. He noticed that the gate was tended by a couple guards, but they were actually dozing at their post. By the time the guards awakened enough to realize an intruder was upon them, it was too late. Joab grabbed one of their swords and quickly disembodied their spirits.

He looked around. Everyone was still sleeping. Nobody had been awakened when he quietly killed the guards. *Good.*

Stepping over to the gate, he began to scrutinize its lock mechanism. *How does this thing work? A light right now would sure be nice.* He had to figure out how to unlock the gate. The gate area was covered and dark, and it was taking him way too long to decipher the mechanism. He felt his way feverishly over the metal and bars.

Ah, this must be it. I need to move this bar. As he pulled the lever, the bar made a strident squeaking noise. To Joab, who was attempting a covert operation in the middle of the night, it sounded like a shrill scream. Metal ground upon metal. He was advertising his presence to the entire population of the stronghold!

But it was too late to hush up now, so he kicked into a faster gear. He had to open this gate. He kept pushing on the metal bar.

Suddenly, he heard voices behind him. Somebody had been awakened by the noisy gate. And they were calling out, "Hello! What's going on over there?"

Adrenalin rushed through his veins. Realizing he had but moments to spare, he pushed with all his might on the bar, and suddenly the entire mechanism gave way. With one great shove, the large gate of Zion began to open.

"Hey! Somebody's opening the gate!" A cry of alarm was being sounded by a Jebusite who realized what was happening.

But it was too little, too late. The gate was open. A group of Israelite soldiers had been watching for the gate to move, and immediately they propped the gate fully open. One of them blew a battle trumpet. Suddenly, the entire Israelite army arose from their places of hiding, and at 2:05 a.m., they all poured swiftly into the stronghold of Zion.

A few of the braver Jebusites attempted a fight and were quickly neutralized. Most of the inhabitants, however, surrendered without a fight. Within minutes, the entire stronghold was subdued.

For Joab, capturing Zion was grueling; for everyone else, it was cake. That is why we could call Joab a forerunner. A forerunner pays a torturous price so that others, who would have never even attempted the tunnels and water shaft, are now able to enter into spiritual exploits.

The Forerunner Role

Joab didn't take the stronghold of Zion; he simply opened the gate from the inside so that the army could enter and take the stronghold.

Joab could have never taken the stronghold alone. He

needed the army to fulfill its role. For the stronghold to be defeated, it was necessary for a forerunner like Joab to go before and open the gate from the inside. But it was equally necessary for the army to be waiting and ready to advance once the gate was opened.

This forerunner principle still applies today. As I have read about healing revivals of the past, many of them began in a similar way. The story often reads something like this: God apprehends a man or woman with a vision and calling for divine healing; that person labors in prayer and the Spirit for divine healing to break out; many people are prayed for, but initially there is little or no evidence of God's healing power; but God's man or woman does not relent from contending for divine breakthrough. Then suddenly it happens. Through a divinely ordained set of circumstances, someone is supernaturally healed. That miracle becomes a gate-opening event. Thereafter, healings begin to break out in abundance. One miracle opens the way for many others to follow.

That is what Joab did. He opened the gate, making a way so that many captives could follow him through that gate and be set free.

The apostle Peter experienced this same dynamic. When he went to the town of Lydda and preached the gospel, there was not much indication of spiritual activity taking place. But suddenly a gate in the Spirit opened up and a paralytic named Aeneas was instantly healed and raised from his sick bed (see Acts 9:32-35). When that notable miracle took place, people turned to the Lord en masse. The healing of Aeneas was a gate-opening event that blew the entire region wide open, spiritually speaking, for the reception of the gospel.

Recognizing that a notable miracle is sometimes the catalyst God uses to break open the stronghold of infirmity, it seems that each geographical area must contend for its own breakthrough. In other words, if the stronghold is penetrated and taken in a city such as Dallas, that does not necessarily mean that the same breakthrough will happen simultaneously in a city such as Houston; Houston may have to contend for itself against its own stronghold of infirmity.

When a stronghold collapses and miracles begin to happen popcorn-style, the potential for kingdom impact grows significantly. We see this in the record of Christ's healing ministry: "...and Jerusalem and Idumea and beyond the Jordan; and those from Tyre and Sidon, a great multitude, when they heard how many things He was doing, came to Him" (Mark 3:8). The thing that drew the masses to Christ was "how many things He was doing." In other words, people were drawn not simply by the *kinds* of miracles that were being performed, but the sheer *number* of miracles that were taking place.

When the sound rang out that *everyone* was being healed, the entire nation was shaken. The poor flocked to Jesus in throngs. We carry the hope that the same thing can happen again. Our hope is that when the gate to the stronghold is opened from the inside, it will be followed by so many notable miracles that the impact for the kingdom will increase exponentially. A great revival will shake the nations, and the way will be prepared for Jesus to return on the clouds of heaven.

Our vision for this great, end-time outpouring of the Spirit is what strengthens us to continue contending for healing even when nothing seems to happen. We are going to keep on praying and keep on knocking. Why? All it takes is for one gate to be opened. When a door of healing opens, it may open at the same time to multitudes.

Clearly, *somebody* has to ascend the water shaft. A forerunner must do the grueling legwork to penetrate and open the stronghold so that others can take over enemy territory.

Opened From the Inside

If you have a pen handy, underline this: Joab opened the stronghold from the inside.

Kingdom doors are often unlocked from the inside. What I mean is, the key to unlocking enemy strongholds is often found by going inside—into the heart of the Holy Spirit who abides within us.

To say it another way, strongholds are usually opened through the internal disciplines of intimacy with God, prayer, fasting, and immersion in the word of God. When Joab navigated the tunnel and water shaft, he was a picture of how we press into the heart of God through intercession in order to touch overcoming power.

Go inside. Go deep into the God who lives within you.

Develop your interior life in God. Pursue communion with the Holy Spirit (2 Corinthians 13:14). Discover the mighty power that resides within you (Romans 8:11). As you go deep in God, the Holy Spirit will show you how to open the gate to the stronghold before you.

One reason this principle encourages my heart is because I have been a prisoner of affliction for many years, and if I thought my release from this stronghold was dependent upon someone else finding a way to get me out, I might become easily discouraged. It would be easy to think, "If my release is dependent upon others, I'm never going to get out of here."

But when I saw that the door is opened from the *inside*, I realized that even I, as a prisoner, have the potential in grace to open the gate.

My point here is that believers need not feel helpless to tackle their strongholds. Every one of us can go deep in God, put down roots in the Spirit and in the word, and believe that God will help us unlock the gate that keeps the prisoners in their cells.

If the gate is opened from the inside, then all are equal candidates for this mission.

I am not waiting for you to come and loose me from the shackles of my affliction. I am going deep in God *now*, for myself. I am groping for that water shaft. I bless you in your search, and I certainly pray that you find it before I do. But I am not waiting for you. I am after it myself, both for my sake and for all the prisoners in the body of Christ.

Prisoners are Not Helpless

When you are a prisoner in a stronghold of affliction, you feel utterly helpless. But your feelings are not exactly telling you the whole truth. The truth is, you can grope your way up the water shaft just as much as Joab or anyone else.

In looking at the prisoners of the Bible who escaped, it is amazing to consider how many times they were delivered, not because someone else prayed for them, but because they themselves pursued an interior life in the Spirit.

For starters, I think of the ultimate prisoner in the Bible— Joseph. Joseph did not get out of his prison because someone else busted through the gates and delivered him; he got out because he developed such a vibrant inner life in God that he was able to hear God in critical moments. That living relationship with God enabled him to give the butler, baker, and then later the king, spot-on interpretations to their dreams (Genesis 40-41). The thing that opened his prison door was the anointing he cultivated in his spirit through prayer. His cell was opened from the inside.

Job was another prisoner who found himself in a horrible stronghold of loss and infirmity. Like Joseph, he did not get out of his prison because someone came along and prayed him through. He got out because of the intimacy with God that he developed in his trial.

David is someone else in the Bible who wrongfully endured great affliction and suffering. For years he ran for his life, living for extended periods in a wilderness place called "the stronghold" (1 Samuel 22:4; 24:22). It was probably a mountain surrounded by steep walls that provided natural protection from Saul's forces. David did not get out of that wilderness because someone came along and delivered him out of Saul's hand; he got out because of the favor he nurtured with God through intimacy (Psalm 18:19). His confinement was opened from the inside.

We could cite similar stories by others in the Bible who ended up in prison strongholds, such as Peter, Paul, and Silas. The common denominator in many of these prison stories is that the key to their release was actually in their—the prisoners'—hands. Through prayer and intimacy, their prison gates were opened from the inside (see, for example, Acts 12:3-17 and 16:25-26).

The prisoner of the Lord, therefore, is not without options. You can go deep in God now and cultivate the kind of intimate relationship with God that has the power to open the doors of your prison. Don't wait for anyone else—go for the water shaft!

Part Two

*Spiritual Applications
for Our Lives*

9

Take Your Stronghold!

"To him who overcomes I will grant to sit with Me on My throne, as I also overcame and sat down with My Father on His throne" (Revelation 3:21).

The Greeks have a fascinating fable about how they conquered the city of Troy. As the myth is told, they were unable to topple the city of Troy (located in modern Turkey) despite a ten-year siege. A brilliant idea led to the collapse of the city. They constructed a huge wooden horse on wheels, perhaps as an alleged battering ram, and placed it near the city. In a sign of defeat, one day the Greek forces packed up and sailed away. Hidden inside an inner compartment of the horse's belly, however, were thirty Greek soldiers.

After watching the Greeks depart, the people of Troy pulled the horse into their city as a victory trophy. That night, however, the Greek soldiers crept out of the horse and opened the gates of the city from the inside. The Greek army had circled back under the cover of night and, once the gates were opened, they swarmed the city of Troy and pillaged it.

The story of how Troy was taken in this mythical war has such strong imagery that it continues to be told to children today. Its intrigue lies in the way the Greeks opened the gates of Troy from the inside—just like the taking of Zion.

This picture helps us visualize how we are going to subdue our stronghold. We must find a way to go deep, get inside, and open the stronghold from within.

Now that we have come to Part Two, I want us to look at spiritual principles that will instruct and equip us to go deep in God and unlock our stronghold from the inside. For starters, let us begin with the apostle John.

John's Stronghold Became a Doorway

In his latter years, the apostle John became a captive in a stronghold called the prison island of Patmos. I would like to show how his exploit of overcoming his prison stronghold was similar to how Joab took Zion.

At the time of this story, John was around ninety years old. He was exiled on the island of Patmos by the Romans because of his resolve to preach the word and give testimony to the gospel of Jesus Christ. It was during this captivity that he wrote these words:

> *I, John, both your brother and companion in the tribulation and kingdom and patience of Jesus Christ, was on the island that is called Patmos for the word of God and for the testimony of Jesus Christ.* **I was in the Spirit on the Lord's Day,** *and I heard behind me a loud voice, as of a trumpet (Revelation 1:9-10).*

John does not tell us how harsh the conditions were on the island or how austere his accommodations. But since Patmos was a prison colony, we can assume living conditions were severe. If I were in John's shoes—ninety and on that island—I reckon I would be tempted to think, "I don't need this. I'm too old for this stuff. Isn't it somebody else's turn to be afflicted? Will I ever have enough tenure in the kingdom to be exempt from this kind of pain and inconvenience?"

The temptation for self-pity was surely present, but John refused to succumb. When the Lord's Day rolled around, he was doing what had become his daily routine—he was in prayer and going deep "in the Spirit."

If ever there was a day that could have gotten him feeling sorry for himself, it would have been the Lord's Day. Because the Lord's Day (being Sunday, the first day of the week, when Jesus rose from the dead) was a celebration of the victorious resurrection of Christ from the dead. Everything about the Lord's Day rang with the promise of life and resurrection power. On a day especially designed by the Lord to promote the release of resurrection life, John was experiencing the total opposite. His body and soul were encompassed by the tentacles of death. Instead of feeling like his body was experiencing resurrection power on the Lord's Day, he was feeling achy, feeble, uncomfortable, unwashed, stiff, tired, and hungry.

And yet, where do we find John on the Lord's Day? Depressed because his faith did not change his circumstances? After all, he was the one who wrote, "As He is, so are we in this world" (1 John 4:17), but that verse did not seem to fit his prison. While the resurrected Christ was seated in glory, John was draped in distress and pain. Do we find him despondent over the disconnection between his state and "as He is"? No, we find him setting all that aside and going deep in the Spirit through prayer. Prison gave him few options, but he was doing the one thing captivity did allow—he was praying. He was pressing into the Holy Spirit in intimacy and communion. And suddenly God visited him and lifted him to another realm. John described his vision in this way:

> *After these things I looked, and behold, a door standing open in heaven. And the first voice which I heard was like a trumpet speaking with me, saying, "Come up here, and I will show you things which must take place after this."* **Immediately I was in the Spirit**; *and behold, a throne set in heaven, and One sat on the throne (Revelation 4:1-2).*

Notice that John said, "I was in the Spirit." Those are the same words he used in Revelation 1:10 to describe how he was praying on the Lord's Day. But his being "in the Spirit" here in Revelation 4:2 is profoundly different from his being "in the Spirit" back in Revelation 1:10. These were two entirely different levels of encounter with God, even though identical words describe both situations. Let us look at the difference.

Level One: John was "in the Spirit" (Revelation 1:10) in the way every believer should be, every day. John simply means that he was praying in the Spirit, giving his love to the Lord, ministering to Him, and listening for the Lord's voice. He was not in a trance but in the body, on the island of Patmos, and totally aware of his surroundings. The Spirit of God was touching his heart and he was feeling the Lord's presence. John entered into this level of the Spirit through his own intentional initiative in prayer.

Level Two: When John says he was "in the Spirit" in Revelation 4:2, he means that he was transported by the Spirit of God to a heavenly realm. He was literally caught up to the throne of God. John was helpless to enter this dimension on his own. The only way to access the glory of the throne room was through divine intervention.

It is one thing to be in the Spirit; it's quite another to be *in the Spirit!*

Said another way, it is one thing to get "in the Spirit" through prayer in the regular, everyday sense; it is another thing altogether to be caught up "in the Spirit" to the realms of glory where encounters with God shape the course of human history.

John was faithful to do what he could do (get in the Spirit), and then God was gracious to do for John what he could not do for himself (get him in the Spirit).

Here is what I want you to see. When John placed himself in the realms of the Spirit that he *could* access, God lifted him into realms that he *could not* access. By getting "in the Spirit" John was inadvertently making himself a candidate to be caught up "in the Spirit."

The same is true for you in the restriction of your stronghold. As you get in the Spirit every day through prayer, you make yourself available for God to lift you in the Spirit and take you to heavenly realms where encounters with the glory of God rewrite human history and determine the course of God's end-time purposes in the earth.

John's stronghold was not hugely different from Joab's. And John handled his much the same way as Joab. He decided to go deep in God and get in the Spirit. As he went deep in the Spirit, a door was opened from inside to the stronghold, and he entered through that door into heavenly realms. Once he stepped through that door, John had an encounter with God of earth-shaking, seismic proportions. The revelation of Christ he received in that encounter produced a book (the book of Revelation) that changed the face of Christianity.

I bet the devil regretted the day he consigned John to that island stronghold. A demonic stronghold was turned into a mighty kingdom gateway. The divine download John received dealt a monumental death blow to Satan's end-time schemes by exposing them openly and revealing God's consummate designs for our planet. A demonic stronghold became a place of divine encounter because an elderly captive decided to go deep in God.

Your stronghold extends to you the same divine invitation to go deep in God and contend for a history-making door to be opened in the Spirit.

Weapons of Our Warfare

Paul affirmed that "the weapons of our warfare are not carnal but mighty in God for pulling down strongholds" (2 Corinthians 10:4). We want to master all of these spiritual weapons listed below in order to excel in pulling down strongholds.

- The word of God
  (which in Ephesians 6:17 is called "the sword of the Spirit" and is used in conjunction with the protective armor of Ephesians 6:14-17)

- The blood of Jesus
  ("And they overcame him by the blood of the Lamb"—Revelation 12:11)

- The word of our testimony
  ("And they overcame him by…the word of their testimony"—Revelation 12:11)

- The laying down of our lives
  ("And they overcame him…and they did not love their lives to the death"—Revelation 12:11)

- The name of Jesus
  ("'And His name, through faith in His name, has made this man strong, whom you see and know. Yes, the faith which comes through Him has given him this perfect soundness in the presence of you all'"—Acts 3:16)

- The word of faith
  ("'For assuredly, I say to you, whoever says to this mountain, "Be removed and be cast into the sea," and does not doubt in his heart, but believes that those

things he says will be done, he will have whatever he says'"—Mark 11:23)

- The gifts of the Spirit
  (see 1 Corinthians 12:7-11)

- The fruit of the Spirit
  (see Galatians 5:22-23)

- Praying in the Holy Spirit
  (when Paul detailed the armor of the believer he closed that section on spiritual warfare with Ephesians 6:18, "praying always with all prayer and supplication in the Spirit")

As you press deep into the heart of God, ask Him for grace to wield every weapon of warfare masterfully.

The Ramifications in This Age

Set your heart on conquering your stronghold here, in this life. You want to take your stronghold on this side of eternity for two reasons. First, kingdom conquests made in this life produce great blessings in this life. Taking the stronghold is far from your last conquest; rather, it is a qualifying feat that enables you to apprehend new vistas of kingdom authority and blessing.

There is a passage in the book of Zechariah that illustrates this truth powerfully. The metaphor in Zechariah is not that of a stronghold but a mountain. But the meaning of the passage is equivalent, whether we see the challenge before us as a stronghold or a mountain.

> *So he answered and said to me: "This is the word of the LORD to Zerubbabel: 'Not by might nor by power, but by My Spirit,' says the LORD of hosts. 'Who are you, O great mountain? Before Zerubbabel you shall become a plain! And he shall bring forth the capstone with shouts of "Grace, grace to it!"'" (Zechariah 4:6-7).*

Notice that the Lord addresses the mountain that resists you as a *Who*, not a *What*. "*Who* are you, O great mountain?" That's because the mountain that hinders your destiny in God rises before you in such ominous reality that it takes on a persona all its own. Your mountain is so identifiable that sometimes you can even assign a name to it. Sometimes it is even energized by a specific principality of darkness. It is no longer a *what* but a *who*. The Lord looks at that mountain and declares, "You shall be leveled into a plain."

The passage contrasts a great mountain with a plain. The contrast between a mountain and a plain can be seen starkly in many American cities such as Denver, Albuquerque, Salt Lake City, Colorado Springs, Phoenix, and El Paso.

Denver is a classic example of the contrast. Denver is a city built on a vast, flat plain. When you are on the plain, you have houses, highways, businesses, schools, restaurants, banks, industry, agriculture, and millions of bustling people. Then go west and you cross an invisible line where the plain stops and the mountain suddenly starts. It goes directly—boom—from plain to mountain. The abruptness of the change is striking.

When you hit that mountain, everything stops. The highways thin out, the banks stop, the schools stop, the restaurants stop, the houses almost totally disappear. While you are climbing the mountain the signs of civilization become very sparse until you come to another hilltop or level area. You do have that occasional hunting cabin, mind you, that is built on the side of a mountain. But for the most part, activity stops when you get to the mountain—which is why the mountain represents wilderness, loneliness, obstacle, challenge, difficulty, resistance, adversity, darkness, morbidity, austerity, and foreboding gloom.

The word of the Lord to Zerubbabel reveals what God wants to do with your mountain. He wants that great obstacle you face—that great mountain—to become a plain. He wants to level that great mountain that resists His will in your life so that what was once foreboding and barren is turned into a fruitful plain. Now a needy generation will be nurtured from the goodness of what God has done in your life.

There *was* a great mountain that God turned into a plain. I am thinking right now of the most morbid, desolate, depressing mountain of all time: Mount Calvary. God took the lonely, gloomy mountain of Calvary, leveled it, and turned it into a fruitful plain that now feeds an entire planet on the goodness of God's salvation.

How do you turn a morbid mountain like Calvary into a fruitful plain? I will tell you how. """Not by might nor by power, but by My Spirit," says the LORD of hosts.'" The only way to turn that kind of mountain into a plain is by going deep into the Spirit. That is what Jesus did in His sufferings, and that is what He is teaching you to do in the face of your mountain.

Allow me to explain the context of Zechariah 4:6-7. The mountain that Zerubbabel was facing was the challenge of building the Lord's temple in Jerusalem at a time when resources were depressingly limited and enemies were energetically resistant. But God assured Zerubbabel that the mountain (i.e., a daunting building project) would be turned into a plain (i.e., the temple would be completed). God confirmed His intent by predicting that the capstone (which was the final stone to be placed in the building) would be put in place by Zerubbabel himself, while shouting "Grace, grace to it!" over the capstone and the completed temple.

I want you to notice: "Grace" was not shouted to the mountain (the challenging building project), but to the plain (the completed temple). Once the mountain had been turned into a plain, then shouts of "Grace!" were declared over the completed temple. Why? Because when the temple was completed, that did not represent the end of the story, but rather the beginning of an altogether new chapter. "Grace!" was shouted over the plain because now the plain had to be developed.

Once the mountain had been turned into a plain, a city now needed to be built. Such a massive undertaking required much grace! Leveling the mountain was only the beginning. The task became to cultivate the newly-formed plain and develop it into a feeder of nations and generations.

This is why you must conquer your mountain-stronghold in this life. Because when you do, the greatness of God's salvation demonstrated through you becomes the basis for feeding an entire generation on the goodness of God. In this age. Here and now. In this life.

The Ramifications in the Age to Come

The second reason to take your stronghold here, in this life, is because of the blessings and kingdom conquests that will follow in the Millennial Kingdom and beyond. When you are victorious in conquering the stronghold before you, you qualify as an overcomer for your *real* destiny in the age to come.

Yes, there will be rewards for your victory in this age; but this age is only your internship, or training ground. This present life is an 80-year internship intended by the Lord to prepare us for our 1,000-year calling in the Millennial Kingdom, then our ultimate destiny in the Eternal State. None of us enters our destiny in this life; this life is only preparatory for our actual destiny.

When Jesus took on the stronghold of hell and death, His eyes were on His destiny in the age to come. He knew that once He prevailed, He would qualify for a greater inheritance in the Millennial Kingdom. Christ's greater destiny in the age to come is the theme of the following passage.

> *Revelation 5:1 And I saw in the right hand of Him who sat on the throne a scroll written inside and on the back, sealed with seven seals. 2 Then I saw a strong angel proclaiming with a loud voice, "Who is worthy to open the scroll and to loose its seals?" 3 And no one in heaven or on the earth or under the earth was able to open the scroll, or to look at it. 4 So I wept much, because no one was found worthy to open and read the scroll, or to look at it. 5 But one of the elders said to me, "Do not weep. Behold, the Lion of the tribe of Judah, the Root of David, has prevailed to open the scroll and to loose its seven seals." 6 And I looked, and behold, in the midst of the throne and of the four living creatures, and in the midst of the elders, stood a Lamb as though it had been slain, having seven horns and seven eyes, which are the seven Spirits of God sent out into all the earth. 7 Then He came and took the scroll out of the right hand of Him who sat on the throne.*

In verse five, one the elders declared that Jesus "prevailed" to open the scroll and loose its seals. The great challenge for Christ at the cross was that He *prevail* over it. Once He prevailed over the cross and hell and the grave, He would qualify (be found worthy) to open the seals on the scroll of His destiny in God.

The same is true for us. God has written a scroll for each one of us that represents our divine destiny in the age to come.

If we "prevail" in this life, we will be "found worthy" to open the Father's scroll which contains our fullest destiny in the age to come. This is why it is essential that we prevail over the stronghold before us. When we go deep in God and unlock the stronghold from the inside, we qualify to open the scroll of the Father's destiny for our lives.

This is the ultimate motivation for overcoming in this life. More than anything else, we desire the glorious adventure of entering into our rightful role in the eternal city. We covet the intimacy of partnering with Jesus forever as He develops His ever-increasing kingdom!

> *Of the **increase** of His government and peace there will be no end, upon the throne of David and over His kingdom, to order it and establish it with judgment and justice from that time forward, even forever. The zeal of the Lord of hosts will perform this (Isaiah 9:7).*

> *"To him who **overcomes** I will grant to sit with Me on My throne, as **I also overcame** and sat down with My Father on His throne" (Revelation 3:21).*

10

Pursuing the Inner Life
of the Holy Spirit

Praying always with all prayer and supplication
in the Spirit (Ephesians 6:18).

When Joab tackled the underground tunnel system beneath Zion, he had to go deep and he had to get immersed. These things speak to us of our need to be filled with the Holy Spirit and to reach, internally, into the glorious depths of His purposes and power. As we are joined to the Holy Spirit in prayer, we connect with the power that opens strongholds from the inside.

This journey of the believer into the interior life of the Spirit is portrayed by Joab at Zion, but is pictured even more graphically and gloriously in Christ's death and resurrection. Let's look at that for a moment.

Christ's final cry on the cross was, "'Father, "into Your hands I commit My spirit"'" (Luke 23:46). Upon that utterance, He breathed His last. But instead of being caught up into the embrace of His Father, He found Himself descending immediately into hell.[1]

Suddenly, Jesus found Himself in the ultimate stronghold. How was He to overcome the stronghold of death? The same way we overcome our stronghold. Hell is opened from the inside.

---

1 Sometimes the same thing happens to us. Sometimes it's after our greatest altars of consecration and abandonment to God that we find ourselves sinking into some of the darkest valleys of life. This is but a test of our faith. The pit is not intended to be the end of your story. God wants you to discover the same power of ascension that Jesus found when He resurrected from the pit of hell.

Inasmuch then as the children have partaken of flesh and blood, He Himself likewise shared in the same, that through death He might destroy him who had the power of death, that is, the devil, and release those who through fear of death were all their lifetime subject to bondage (Hebrews 2:14-15).

Jesus had to go inside death to destroy death and the devil. However, He chose, for strategic reasons, to extend Satan's lease and postpone the enforcement of his destruction. Why? Because God has a purpose for keeping Satan in the fray. Whenever Satan erects a scheme against us, we have the opportunity to learn warfare by engaging the stronghold. We grow in the process and gain the joy of enforcing Christ's victory at His side.

These two passages describe Christ's warfare in hell:

"When a strong man, fully armed, guards his own palace, his goods are in peace. But when a stronger than he comes upon him and overcomes him, he takes from him all his armor in which he trusted, and divides his spoils" (Luke 11:21-22).

Having disarmed principalities and powers, He made a public spectacle of them, triumphing over them in it (Colossians 2:15).

Through the cross and resurrection, Jesus overcame Satan, stripped him of all his armor, and plundered his stronghold. Jesus paid the price for all the captives of infirmity to be healed and released. When we engage strongholds of infirmity today, we are simply enforcing the victory that Jesus effected over Satan at Calvary. Jesus now invites us to share in His triumph over all the works of darkness. Now it is our turn. We are learning to plunder Satan's goods Jesus-style.

Jesus needed the help of the Holy Spirit to overcome the stronghold of death. This is what Romans 1:4 means when it says that Jesus was resurrected from the dead "according to the Spirit of holiness." Jesus went inside, into the power of the Holy Spirit, and through that power opened up the gates of hell from the inside. Once He had broken through hell's gates, He was able to lead forth from the corridors of death many captives who had been held by Sheol (Ephesians 4:8-10).

Jesus is our pattern. He entered the stronghold of death

and opened the gates of hell from the inside by the power of the Holy Spirit. We overcome by following in His steps. He will show us how to open our stronghold from the inside through the power of that same Holy Spirit.

The Helper

Jesus told us the Holy Spirit was given to us as our Helper (John 14:16, 26; 15:26; 16:7). He is an amazingly capable Helper. When Jesus was on the cross, the Holy Spirit enabled Jesus to endure the utter agony of His impalement and complete the course of His sufferings right up to the point of death (Hebrews 9:14). He also helped the Father take the fullness of His wrath against sin and empty it upon His Son (as inferred by Hebrews 9:14). The extravagant extremity of the cross could be consummated only through the ministration of the Helper. That Holy Spirit, who helped the Father and the Son conquer Mount Calvary, is the same Helper who empowers you to overcome your stronghold. Given His hefty portfolio of previous successes, you could not ask for better support.

You're in good hands with the Helper.

Some believers think they need help or guidance to navigate the interior life of the Holy Spirit. So they look for a book or study guide or mentor to show them how to access the power of the Holy Spirit. Seeking such aids is not necessarily wrong, but it can be superfluous. Let me illustrate what I mean in computer terms.

Computers usually come with a Help program. The Help program is designed to enable users to figure out how to navigate and use all the features of the computer. I would be willing to bet that almost no one reading this chapter has ever called the manufacturer of their computer and asked for help to understand their Help program. Why not? Because the Help program is designed to be self-explanatory. If you need help to understand a Help program, it is no longer a help. Asking for help with a Help program is ironic and redundant because a Help program *is* your source of help.

The same is true of the Holy Spirit. You do not need a guide to the Holy Spirit. You do not need a manual or book to teach you how to access the Holy Spirit's assistance.

You don't need help with the Helper. The Holy Spirit is all

the help you need!

Someone might wonder, "How do I access, then, the power of the Holy Spirit?" Answer: You just go to the Holy Spirit and cry out, "Help!" When you call, He is immediately present in your time of need.

I have decided that if the Holy Spirit was enough for Jesus at Calvary, then He is enough for me, too. I do not need another. He is all the help I need. "Therefore I will call upon Him as long as I live" (Psalm 116:2).

If I can't get it with the Holy Spirit's help, I reckon I don't need it.

The first step, therefore, to going deep in the Holy Spirit is to call for help. Ask Him to guide and show you the way. "Holy Spirit, how am I going to access this water shaft? How am I going to penetrate this stronghold? How do I open this thing from the inside?" Offer up that prayer and then begin to pray in the Spirit. He knows the way, and He will take you on the journey of discovering how to navigate this terrain.

Now I want to explain how our connection to the Holy Spirit is the basis for our power in spiritual warfare.

Power Through the Holy Spirit

The Holy Spirit has been given to us so that we might access the power of God. While it is true that we can touch God's power by relating to the Father or to the Son, the Holy Spirit was assigned to us specifically by Jesus to help us connect with the power of God. Let me back up and explain what I mean.

During His earthly ministry, Jesus gave His disciples power and authority to cast out unclean spirits and to heal all kinds of sickness and disease.

> And when He had called His twelve disciples to Him, He gave them power over unclean spirits, to cast them out, and to heal all kinds of sickness and all kinds of disease (Matthew 10:1).

He did not give them this authority for just one day or one set of meetings; it remained with them for an extended season. They operated under it quite possibly for as long as three years.

But then they lost the power He gave them in Matthew 10:1. I say they lost it because, later on, Jesus came back to them and said, "You will receive power."

> *"But you shall receive power when the Holy Spirit has come*
> *upon you; and you shall be witnesses to Me in Jerusalem,*
> *and in all Judea and Samaria, and to the end of the earth"*
> *(Acts 1:8).*

By saying a second time that they would receive power, He was inferring that they had lost what He gave them the first time around in Matthew 10:1. This leaves us wondering: When did they lose the power He first gave them?

I believe they lost their initial power over unclean spirits and diseases when Jesus died on the cross. Here is why I say that. The basis of their power was the bodily presence of Christ. As long as He was physically with them, they could function in the authority He gave them. But when He died, they lost their power over sickness and disease because He was no longer present in the body. The basis for their power was suddenly taken away.

After His resurrection, however, Jesus wanted to assure them that He still desired for them to function in power and authority over unclean spirits and diseases. So He told them the power to heal and deliver would be given a second time. The basis for their power this second time, however, would be different. It would no longer be based upon His bodily presence (since He was about to ascend to the Father). The basis of their power over unclean spirits would now be their connection to the Holy Spirit. This is what He meant when He said, "'But you shall receive power when the Holy Spirit has come upon you'" (Acts 1:8).

On the Day of Pentecost, the disciples received a fresh infusion of power (Acts 2). That fact is proven in the book of Acts by the way they cast out demons and healed the sick. Their source of authority was the resident Holy Spirit who had filled and saturated them.

The agency of power for believers today remains exactly the same. The basis of our power is a real, vital connection to the Holy Spirit. When He abides within, He empowers us with the glory of His fullness. Through the Holy Spirit, we receive the same power over sickness that Jesus gave His disciples when He was physically with them. The only difference is that now its basis is a dynamic, vital relationship with the Holy Spirit.

Smith Wigglesworth, the great healing evangelist, once said,

> I am never happier in the Lord than when I am in a
> bedroom with a sick person. I have had more revela-
> tions of the Lord's presence when I have ministered to
> the sick at their bedsides than at any other time. It is as
> your heart goes out to the needy ones in deep compas-
> sion that the Lord manifests His presence. You are able
> to locate their position. It is then that you know that
> you must be filled with the Spirit to deal with the con-
> ditions before you.[2]

Wigglesworth's experience demonstrated why we eagerly
desire to walk in cadence with the Holy Spirit. We know, as we
are filled to overflowing with the Holy Spirit, that we will experience power over the strongholds before us—over unclean
spirits and sicknesses. And we know that this power is ours
continually—for as long as we remain tethered to the Holy
Spirit in a real, dynamic, fiery relationship of love.

Right now, as I write this, my connection to the Holy Spirit
is not producing the kind of power Jesus demonstrated. But this
does not discourage me. Rather, I see myself like Joab, pressing
and pushing my way through interior passageways. The gate
has not yet opened, but I am pressing into the Holy Spirit with
unrelenting tenacity, confident that He will direct my pursuit.

Groaning in the Holy Spirit

One of the ways we encounter the power of the Holy Spirit
is through His intercessory ministry. The Holy Spirit desires to
make intercession for us—He wants to be our advocate. One
of our first priorities in seeking more of the Spirit, therefore, is
learning to engage and release His intercessory ministry on our
behalf. Here's the passage that reveals this aspect of the Holy
Spirit's ministry.

> *Likewise the Spirit also helps in our weaknesses. For we do
> not know what we should pray for as we ought, but the Spirit
> Himself makes intercession for us with groanings which can-
> not be uttered. Now He who searches the hearts knows what*

---

2   Smith Wigglesworth, *Ever Increasing Faith.* Gospel Publishing House,
     Springfield, MO, 1924, p. 131.

> *the mind of the Spirit is, because He makes intercession for*
> *the saints according to the will of God (Romans 8:26-27).*

Question: Who releases the "groanings which cannot be uttered"? Does the Holy Spirit express these groanings in heaven totally independently of us? Does He pray for us while we are not even aware of it and busily going about the affairs of our day?

No. These groanings are not expressed by the Holy Spirit somewhere in the heavenlies. Rather, these groanings are expressed through *us*. We are the channel. As we give ourselves to prayer, there is a kind of praying in which the Holy Spirit prays and groans through us.

The first point to emphasize from this passage, therefore, is that the Holy Spirit prays *through* us.

Please get this: If we become the channel, the Holy Spirit will groan through us. If we do not actively invoke Him to pray through us, this intercessory ministry of the Holy Spirit *does not happen*. He does not groan independently of us. In other words, He does not groan for us regardless of what we do. He prays for us only as we come aside and actively engage Him and become the conduit of His groanings.

I do not mean that the Holy Spirit does nothing for us until we enter into His groanings. The Holy Spirit is intensely active in our lives twenty-four hours a day. However, as it regards His groaning intercessions, that particular aspect of His ministry happens only through our active initiative.

Either the groaning happens *through* us or it doesn't happen at all.[3]

The second point to emphasize from this passage is that the

3　It may be helpful to explain that the intercessory ministry of the Holy Spirit per Romans 8:26-27 is different from the intercessory ministry of Christ as described in these verses:

It is Christ who died, and furthermore is also risen, who is even at the right hand of God, who also makes intercession for us (Romans 8:34).

Therefore He is also able to save to the uttermost those who come to God through Him, since He always lives to make intercession for them (Hebrews 7:25).

Christ's intercessory ministry happens in heavenly places, before the throne of God, and He is constantly interceding for the saints, even while you are sleeping. In contrast, the Holy Spirit's intercessory ministry happens in and through you, and only when you personally activate it.

Holy Spirit prays *for* us. This is said explicitly in the text: "the Spirit Himself makes intercession for us." Furthermore, when the Holy Spirit prays for us, He prays perfect prayers "according to the will of God" (Romans 8:27). Without a doubt, you want Him praying these kinds of perfect prayers for you!

Here is what I want you to remember from this passage: The Holy Spirit prays *through* us; and when He does, He prays *for* us (Romans 8:26).

Now, there is a kind of praying in which we groan for ourselves. Paul spoke of it just a couple verses earlier in Romans 8.

> *Not only that, but we also who have the firstfruits of the Spirit, even we ourselves groan within ourselves, eagerly waiting for the adoption, the redemption of our body (Romans 8:23).*

Based on this verse, it is fitting that we give much time in groaning prayer for ourselves. *This is us groaning for us.*

Romans 8:26-27 is speaking, however, about an altogether different operation of prayer. This is not us praying for ourselves; this is us allowing the Holy Spirit to pray for us as He groans through us. It is important to distinguish that these are not *our* prayers for us but *His* prayers for us.

The Holy Spirit wants to target the needs of our lives personally in His intercessions. He wants to pray God's will regarding our stronghold. What phenomenally amazing, personal, individual care from the Holy Spirit!

When the Holy Spirit groans through us, His intercessions do not necessarily need to engage our mind. We do not need to understand His groanings in order for them to be valid. All we need to know is that He is praying perfectly for us in the will of God as we release His groanings through our spirit. What a glorious way to know we are praying according to the will of God!

Practical Suggestions

The next time you go to prayer, I invite you to exercise yourself in this dimension of prayer. Start by opening your Bible to Romans 8:26-27. Then simply ask, "Holy Spirit, pray through me right now. Groan through me." Then give yourself to the Spirit's groanings which are too deep for words. Sometimes you will groan audibly, but not always. The groans do not have to be audible to be effective.

Your mind may rest on a specific need in your life, or on something as general as, "Give me the will of God." The Holy Spirit's groanings are not triggered primarily by your mind, however, but by your spirit. You are praying from your belly. The Helper, who resides in the seat of your spirit, is now praying through your spirit. Allow the groans to originate deep within and then release them as the Holy Spirit helps you. He is waiting to groan through you.

When I am exercising myself in the groanings of the Spirit, I find more momentum comes upon my prayers when I work through each phrase of the Lord's Prayer (Matthew 6:9-13). While groaning in this manner, I will sometimes say things like, "Holy Spirit, pray for me. Give me the kingdom. Give me the will of God. Insist upon it, Holy Spirit. Groan me into the will of God." But my focus is not primarily on speaking these kinds of things; my focus is primarily upon groaning the groans of the Holy Spirit.

It is this kind of internal praying that Joab embodied when he entered into the deep in order to open the stronghold from the inside.

Praying like this is essential, therefore, as we set our faces against the stronghold before us. The Holy Spirit will pray perfect prayers about that stronghold if only we will allow Him to groan for us and through us.

I encourage you to explore the depths of the Spirit in prayer. It is one thing to write or talk about going deep in the Spirit in prayer; it is another thing to actually do it. Decide that you are actually going to go there!

Be Filled With the Spirit

Our stronghold will be opened from the inside—as we are completely and totally filled with the Holy Spirit. There are many metaphors in the Bible that illustrate the manner in which the Holy Spirit fills us and works in our lives. Interestingly, many of those metaphors are related to weather: wind, rain, hail, tornadoes (whirlwinds), lightning, thunder, and flooding. One reason for the connection between the Holy Spirit and weather is that when the Spirit moves in our lives,

He administers a change of season. When the power of His Spirit blows, it carries the ability to blow us literally right out of our "stronghold season" and into a season of deliverance and overcoming joy.

This is what happened to Zacharias when he found himself in a "stronghold season" of muteness (Luke 1:5-80). Let me explain.

Zacharias was an elderly priest who was visited by the angel Gabriel while offering incense in the temple. Gabriel told him he would have a miracle son in his old age—who was to be John the Baptist—but Zacharias struggled to believe. He could not help it. He had implored God for decades for a son, yet his prayers were seemingly unheeded. The heartsickness of delayed answers had made his heart crusty and unresponsive to the word of faith, even when offered great promises by Gabriel himself.

Because he did not believe the promise of God, Gabriel told Zacharias that he would be mute until its fulfillment. Sure enough, Zacharias was immediately struck mute, and was unable to speak until John the Baptist was born. It was when Zacharias gave his son the name John that his tongue was suddenly loosed.

When his mouth was opened, it marked a sudden change of seasons in his life and he exploded in an amazing string of prophetic utterances. He began to prophesy about the glories of the Messiah, and he told how his infant son would prepare the way for the Messiah to be revealed. In other words, he prophesied the very things that just ten months earlier he was not able to believe.

When Zacharias entered his stronghold of muteness, he was a crusty old wineskin with a sincere but hardened heart. When he was released from the stronghold ten months later, he emerged a prophetic oracle.

How can we account for such a dramatic transformation in just ten short months? There were three primary factors that contributed to such profound change.

1. Ten months in a stronghold of infirmity.

The ten months Zacharias spent in the stronghold of muteness were absolutely transformational for him. Like Joseph in his prison, Zacharias used the confinement to press into the Holy Spirit for understanding into God's purposes. Zacharias emerged from the crucible with wisdom and understanding that could be gained only by going deep in prayer and in the study of Scripture.

In the same way, God designs for the stronghold you face to be a training ground for greater understanding and depth in God. Don't waste a good prison sentence; use the confinement to press into God in the word and prayer like never before.

2. *Supernatural breakthrough.*

The second thing that transformed Zacharias and turned him into a prophetic oracle was the supernatural gift of a son in his old age. His wife, Elizabeth, was barren throughout their entire marriage, but then in her elderly years she miraculously gave birth to a son. The power of that miracle marked Zacharias.

This is why God wants to do a miracle in your life and bring down the stronghold that hinders your progress in God. The miracle itself will impart something into the fiber of your being that no one will ever be able to take from you. When God performs a miracle on your behalf, it changes your spiritual chemistry. It empowers you with a testimony. It imbues you with boldness before the throne. God will use the dramatic nature of your deliverance to mark you forever with a boldness in the Holy Spirit. You will end your days declaring the goodness of God in the land of the living.

3. *The infilling of the Holy Spirit.*

This was the most powerful contributor to Zacharias's sudden transformation. When his miracle son was born and his tongue was loosed, the Holy Spirit suddenly fell upon him. The biblical record says that he was "filled with the Holy Spirit, and prophesied" (Luke 1:67).

The Holy Spirit will change you more completely and suddenly than you can imagine. He instantly turned Zacharias into a prophesying, faith-pronouncing warrior. *O Holy Spirit, how we want this same infilling!*

"'But you shall receive power when the Holy Spirit has come upon you'" (Acts 1:8). We long to be transformed by this power! Many are the times I have prayed, "Fill me or kill me." I cannot live with anything less than the Spirit's fullness.

When you get the Spirit, you get all of God. The Holy Spirit administrates the fullness of God to the human spirit. When you are filled with the Holy Spirit, you are not getting just one-third of God. When you get the Father, you get all of God; when you get the Son, you get all of God; and when you get the Spirit, you are getting all of God. When you are filled with the Holy Spirit, you are filled with all the fullness of God (Ephesians 3:16-19).

The Lord filled Zacharias with the Holy Spirit when he finally took his stronghold; may the Lord fill you in the same way. May you emerge from your stronghold not only victorious over your adversary, but also declaring the high praises of God and the prophetic oracles of the Lord for your generation.

Amen!

11

Contending for Healing

And the whole multitude sought to touch Him, for power went out from Him and healed them all (Luke 6:19).

I have presented the stronghold of Zion as the stronghold of infirmity and disease that remains largely unchallenged in the church today. We must go after this stronghold! I am writing this chapter, therefore, especially for those who are facing a stronghold related to sickness, infirmity, disease, or affliction. I want to encourage your heart as you pursue a breakthrough in the realm of divine healing.

Let me begin by saying I see two primary principles related to divine healing.

First, it is God's will to heal everyone. There are many impediments and factors that may hinder the release of God's healing power, but when all those factors are removed or satisfied and faith is present, it is always God's will to heal. Jesus proved this by healing everyone that came to Him for healing.

So He touched her hand, and the fever left her. And she arose and served them. When evening had come, they brought to Him many who were demon-possessed. And He cast out the spirits with a word, and healed all who were sick, that it might be fulfilled which was spoken by Isaiah the prophet, saying: "He Himself took our infirmities and bore our sicknesses" (Matthew 8:15-17).

If Jesus had refused to heal even one person who came to Him, He would have undermined the faith of multitudes because many would wonder, "Perhaps I'm the exception, just like that one person Jesus didn't heal." Jesus purposely never permitted that kind of thinking to be validated. He demonstrated that it is always God's will to heal when He has a clear vessel through whom He can work. The only exception to this was the occasion in which Herod brought a sick person to Jesus for healing but Jesus refused (Luke 23:8). The reason was clear, though. In duplicitous insincerity, Herod was seeking carnal entertainment. Whenever someone calls on Jesus in sincerity, healing is always God's perfect and desired outcome.

Jesus created you with ears to hear His voice. He gave you eyes to behold His glory. He gave you a voice so you could speak with Him. He gave you smell to enjoy His fragrance. He gave you touch so you could feel His embrace. He gave you hands so you could serve Him. He gave you feet so you could walk with Him. We need all of our senses, faculties, and members in order to interact fully with Him. Jesus wants you whole so you can relate to Him in wholeness. It is His will to heal and make you whole.

It is as much God's will that all men be healed today as it is His will that all men be saved today. "'Behold, now is the day of salvation'" (2 Corinthians 6:2). It is not God's will that any men perish (2 Peter 3:9), and yet many are perishing. In the same way, it is not God's will that men be sick today and yet many are. That many Christians are not healed today does not negate the fact that God wants them to be healed. Therefore, when you pray for healing, pray and believe for healing *today. Now!* Let every day be a day of expectant prayer. God wants to save and heal you now. If there is a hindrance and you are not healed today, do not be thrown off balance. Get up tomorrow and continue to press into His promised healing. Healing is available through the cross of Christ and it is His will that you receive it.

The second principle is this: God's design is that we contend and persevere in faith until everything that hinders or delays divine healing is satisfied or removed and the healing is manifest. The process involved in contending (repentance, prayer, fasting, self-denial, praise, Scripture study, intimacy with Jesus, good works, spiritual warfare, waiting on the Lord, etc.) is used masterfully by the Lord to change us so profoundly that great kingdom advantage is gained through the fight.

We emerge from the struggle not simply delivered but transformed into deliverers (Obadiah 21).

For this reason, we should never despise the challenge of contending for divine healing. The strenuous nature of climbing the water shaft is sometimes essential in the process. The rigors are used by God to conform us to the meekness of Christ. Jesus, in His sinless perfection, did not need to be changed by such processes; He was a clear vessel through whom God could heal everyone, every time. Our quest is to cooperate with God's grace until we become equally useful vessels in the Master's hand.

Jesus does not only want to heal us, He also wants to change us. That is one reason there can sometimes be a time delay in healing. Healing in itself does not fully satisfy God's desire for our lives. There are many people in hell, for example, who were healed by Jesus in their bodies during their lifetime on earth. Healed, but in hell. Their healing did not insure eternal fruit. Bodily healing is not enough; we must also experience a change in our hearts that produces eternal glory and everlasting fruit. That change sometimes happens by God putting the healing on pause and motivating us to press into Him with fervency. There are few things more life-changing than climbing a difficult water shaft and opening a stronghold from the inside.

To clarify, I am *not* saying that God will use you in power only after you have gone through some arduous, refining process. Not at all! Sometimes God uses newborn believers in glorious demonstrations of power, even though they are very immature in grace. God can use you at any time, at any place. He can sovereignly overstep all impediments and heal simply because someone acted upon Christ's word, "'Ask, and it will be given to you'" (Matthew 7:7). What I *do* mean is that when you have prayed in faith and not seen your stronghold toppled, you should not give up and admit defeat. Stay with it. Engage in the rigors of the quest until the stronghold is opened and taken.

John G. Lake was a man whom God used mightily in the ministry of divine healing around a hundred years ago. Here is a story from his life that I hope will encourage you as you seek to climb the water shaft and take your stronghold.

John G. Lake once had a divine visitation in which an

angel opened the word of God and pointed to Acts 2, which describes the outpouring of the Holy Spirit at Pentecost. According to Lake, the angel said to him, "This is Pentecost as God gave it through the heart of Jesus. Strive for this. Contend for this. Teach the people to pray for this. For this, and this alone, will meet the necessity of the human heart, and this alone will have the power to overcome the forces of darkness. Pray. Pray. Pray. Teach the people to pray. Prayer and prayer alone, much prayer, persistent prayer, is the door of entrance into the heart of God."[1]

This kind of prayer not only unlocks strongholds; it also makes us warriors of another caliber.

Another Clarification

Let me explain about yet another thing that I am *not* meaning to say in this book.

I am *not* saying that if you are sick or afflicted that your only hope for healing is if you can gather the strength to crawl up some dark shaft and valiantly open your own stronghold from the inside. I do not want to give the impression that healing is available only to those who are capable of some kind of heroic spiritual effort.

The fact is that sickness and affliction often have a way of sapping strength from a saint. Infirmity can be so overwhelming to the captive that all one can do sometimes is survive from day to day. If your pain levels are so strong or your strength levels so weak that you are rendered incapable of tackling the stronghold of affliction, then I would comfort you with the assurance of Scripture: "For the LORD...does not despise His prisoners" (Psalm 69:33). God does not despise the weakness and frailty you feel in your imprisonment. He understands. He knows that we are but flesh.

This is why God, in His grace, will raise up other members in the body of Christ to contend for your healing. Then, when you are released, your deliverance will not be a testimony to your resolve or consecration. If your healing is a testimony to your spiritual competence, that is no gospel at all. That is a legalistic testimony that tells others they must measure up

---

1   Godschalk, Liz. *Renewal Journal*, 1995, cited at: http://www.pastornet.
     net.au/renewal/revival/lake.html

to a certain standard of spiritual performance if they are to be healed. That kind of gospel is depressing because no one is good enough to attain it. God wants to heal you in such a way that He is glorified for His grace, goodness, and merciful compassion.

My exhortation to the weak, therefore, is that they simply set their love upon God. And my exhortation to the strong is, fight for the captives! Contend for their release. Fight for those who cannot fight for themselves. Let all the members of the body fulfill their function.

The Wisdom of the Rigor

We might be prone to ask, "Lord, why have You made taking the stronghold so rigorous? Why does it require such all-consuming effort and disciplined focus?"

One of the reasons for the stringency of the pursuit is because the Lord uses it to cultivate within us new dimensions of intimacy with Him. Going after the stronghold demands spiritual violence in the areas of fasting, prayer, meditation in the word, etc. These are the disciplines that cultivate within us the greatest intimacy with Jesus. At the end of the day, we emerge not only with new levels of spiritual authority over afflicting spirits, but we also come up leaning on our Beloved (Song of Solomon 8:5). The wilderness journey of engaging the stronghold has so marked us that we come up from the wilderness enjoying a stronger intimacy with the Lord.

The necessity of this intimacy in the midst of increased spiritual authority cannot be over-emphasized. Herein is one of the greatest principles of Joseph's life. God had destined Joseph for great levels of spiritual authority, but He could not release him into that authority without first establishing him in intimacy. That is what the stronghold of his prison was all about. God used Joseph's captivity to seal his heart in love and devotion so that, when the promotion finally came, Joseph was able to handle the promotion without becoming a casualty. God loved Joseph too much to give him the promotion without the pruning. God not only wanted to make Joseph fruitful; He also wanted to preserve him from self-destructing.[2]

---

2   Solomon is an example of a man who was given the promotion without the pruning and, as a result, he eventually suffered shipwreck.

The same is true for you. God does not want to use you and then lose you. That is why the journey to spiritual authority over strongholds is so strenuous. The intimacy with God that the journey cultivates becomes the very safeguard to preserve the vessel from self-destructing under the pressure of promotion, prominence, and abundance.

This is the protection of intimacy. "'But the people who *know their God* shall be strong, and carry out great exploits'" (Daniel 11:32).

The Captives are Waiting

There are many captives holed up in strongholds of affliction and infirmity and they are waiting for someone to do whatever it takes to free them.

Not everyone is capable of extricating himself from the awful circumstances into which he has fallen. Jesus expressed it this way, "'What man is there among you who has one sheep, and if it falls into a pit on the Sabbath, will not lay hold of it and lift it out?'" (Matthew 12:11). In context, He was actually talking about divine healing. It is possible for a person to fall into a pit of physical affliction from which he or she is incapable of escaping. Someone else must lift them out. Jesus demonstrated this in His healing ministry. Many came to Him who were powerless to lift themselves out of their pits of infirmity, and He healed them all.

The church is full of sheep (believers) who have fallen into a pit of infirmity and are waiting for someone with enough strength in the Spirit to lift them out. It takes a mighty arm to reach down into a pit, lay hold of that person, and lift him or her out. Jesus demonstrated this kind of might, and we are enjoined to be filled with the same kind of spiritual might: "Finally, my brethren, be strong in the Lord and in the power of His might" (Ephesians 6:10). Let us not relent until we have been made, by grace, into rescuers of the fallen. May we become deliverers of men!

On one occasion, Jesus ministered deliverance to a man who was captive to affliction from birth. He had been born blind. The disciples wanted to know if his blindness was because of his sin or his parents' sin. "Jesus answered, 'Neither this man nor his parents sinned, but that the works of God should be revealed in him'" (John 9:3). In other words, he endured that affliction all those years because he was waiting for someone to demonstrate the works of God in his life. Finally the day came for which he had been living—the day he met Jesus and was delivered from his stronghold.

Notice that Jesus said "'the works of God *should* be revealed in him.'" The word "should" is important here. It means that the works of God *ought to* be revealed in this man. It's *only right*. In other words, Jesus made this man's healing an issue of *justice*. The only just thing for this captive of infirmity was that someone should release him so the works of God might be revealed in him.

Jesus made the exact same point when He healed the woman who was bound with a spirit of infirmity for eighteen years. Regarding her healing He said, "'So *ought not* this woman, being a daughter of Abraham, whom Satan has bound—think of it—for eighteen years, be loosed from this bond on the Sabbath?'" (Luke 13:16). By saying "ought not," Jesus inferred that justice demanded this woman's healing. It was only right and just that this daughter of faith, after being bound by Satan in a stronghold of infirmity for eighteen years, be healed on the Sabbath—and *especially* on the Sabbath! A true justice movement is zealous to see the healing of God come to the captives, and all the more when God's people are gathered to their Sabbath convocation.

Yes, healing is an issue of justice. Captives are unjustly being held in demonic strongholds of infirmity, and justice requires that someone scale the water shaft, open the stronghold's gate from the inside, and make way for the release of the captives.

Proverbs 13:23 says, "For lack of justice there is waste." Where justice is lacking—that is, where captives are not delivered from their unjust sufferings—they sit in their strongholds and waste away. The potential of their lives is squandered. Dreams are not merely unrealized, they are crushed and pulverized. Hope and vision are extinguished. The prisoners languish aimlessly. Their lives are an utter waste.

This is why God loves justice (Isaiah 61:8). He loves the justice of healing. When justice brings release to the captives, hope springs alive. This is why the lame, when healed, begin to walk and leap and praise God (Acts 3:8). A life that was wasting away is suddenly able to become fruitful in the kingdom. Gifts and callings once held captive are released into their God-ordained function, bringing praise and glory to God. A barren life is turned into a fruitful garden. What cause for celebration and joy!

When God brings justice to the church by releasing the flow of divine healing, the wastelands of human travesties will be turned into verdant valleys of abundant harvest that testify to the works of God.

Set Your Face

Someone might ask, "How do I go about taking on the stronghold of infirmity? Where do I start?"

One way to start can be found in the words of Psalm 89:23, "'I will beat down his foes before his face.'" In this Scripture, God was saying that as David set his face against his enemies, He would enter into the battle with him and beat down his foes before him.

The principle is this: God will beat down your enemies as you set your face against them.

Set your face against the stronghold of affliction and infirmity. Resolve in your heart to move forward unflinchingly against this fortress of mocking spirits. Turn neither to the left nor right. Place all your focus and resolve upon this one enemy.

Pray for the sick at every turn. Lay your hands on the sick, the disabled, the tormented, and pray for them at every opportunity. Never back away or ease off. Set your face like flint.

As you set your face to overturn the stronghold before you, may the Lord enter into the battle with you and beat down your foes before your face. May the name of the Lord Jesus be glorified through your obedience!

12

Pursuing Faith

But you, O man of God, flee these things and pursue...faith
(1 Timothy 6:11).

We all realize that taking the stronghold before us will require a strong exercise of faith. But faith does not exist naturally on this planet. It is a heavenly quality, and it must be received from heaven if it is to be found on earth. How, then, do we receive stronghold-penetrating faith?

Faith comes from hearing the word of God. "So then faith comes by hearing, and hearing by the word of God" (Romans 10:17). Most of us know the meaning of that verse well. There are two other verses, however, that also explain the source of faith, and these verses are probably not as well known.

> *And the grace of our Lord was exceedingly abundant, with faith and love which are **in Christ Jesus** (1 Timothy 1:14).*

> *"Hold fast the pattern of sound words which you have heard from me, in faith and love which are **in Christ Jesus** (2 Timothy 1:13).*

In both verses, Paul affirmed that faith is "in Christ Jesus." It resides within His person. The way to faith is by clinging feverishly to Jesus, so that the faith that is resident in Him is imparted to us. This is why we pursue spiritual union with Christ, through the word and the Spirit. We want the knowledge of Christ to fill and transform us until the very faith of Christ fills every molecule of our being.

The clinging relationship we have with Jesus is altogether

glorious, but for centuries it was veiled from our understanding. Under the Old Covenant, we understood that *God is with us* (Isaiah 7:14) and that *we are in God* (Psalm 90:1); but it was not until the New Covenant that we realized *God is in us*. Herein is the power of our faith. "Christ in you, the hope of glory" (Colossians 1:27).

As we are joined to Christ, He actually lives within us. When He lives within us, then all the faith that dwells in Him dwells in us too. Now we can reach inside to access all the faith that is in Christ. The door to the faith we seek is opened from the inside.

David's Source of Faith

David was a man of uncommon faith. It was through faith that he took the stronghold of Zion (2 Samuel 5:7). But where did he get the stronghold-destroying faith that was operating in his spirit? We want to understand his source so we can use that same kind of faith against our stronghold.

To understand David's faith, you have to go back to an event in his youth that completely transformed him. It is told in one single verse. It is impossible to properly interpret David's life story without seeing it through the lens of this one verse. Here is that verse.

Then Samuel took the horn of oil and anointed him in the midst of his brothers; and the Spirit of the LORD came upon David from that day forward (1 Samuel 16:13).

When Samuel anointed David with oil as king of Israel, something powerful happened. The anointing changed David forever. The reason for David's faith was the anointing of the Holy Spirit upon his life.

All believers have an anointing from God, according to 1 John 2:27—"But the anointing which you have received from Him abides in you, and you do not need that anyone teach you; but as the same anointing teaches you concerning all things, and is true, and is not a lie, and just as it has taught you, you will abide in Him." This is an anointing that abides "in" the believer.

But the anointing that Samuel poured upon David was

different. It was an anointing of another caliber. It was an anointing that came "upon" him. It remained upon him "from that day forward." I call this a *remaining anointing*, and it changed David profoundly. The faith operating in David's spirit was the direct result of this remaining anointing.

It was this same remaining anointing that came upon Jesus at His baptism. John the Baptist testified that he saw the Spirit descend like a dove and come to rest on Jesus. John said the Holy Spirit "'remained upon Him'" (John 1:32).

When this remaining anointing came upon Jesus, it was for the purpose of empowering Him to fulfill His ministry. Jesus spoke of this anointing when He said,

> *"The Spirit of the LORD is upon Me, because He has anointed Me to preach the gospel to the poor; He has sent Me to heal the brokenhearted, to proclaim liberty to the captives and recovery of sight to the blind, to set at liberty those who are oppressed" (Luke 4:18).*

The remaining anointing carried with it the faith and power Jesus needed to set captives free from their strongholds. This was the same kind of anointing that came upon David. When this remaining anointing came upon David, it filled him with faith and confidence in his God. He was never the same again.

An Anointed Perspective

In the next chapter of David's story (1 Samuel 17), we see how dramatically the anointing changed him. At the time, he was still a youth. Some scholars suggest he was around seventeen years of age.

David was sent by his father to inquire into the welfare of his brothers and bring them some food. They were warriors in Israel's army and so were camped near the line of battle. Every morning and evening, Goliath would stand and call out to the armies of Israel, taunting them and challenging them to a duel. So when David came to see his brothers, he observed for the first time Goliath's rant against the armies of Israel.

David's response to Goliath's challenge was utterly amazing.

> *Then David spoke to the men who stood by him, saying, "What shall be done for the man who kills this Philistine*

and takes away the reproach from Israel? For who is this un-
circumcised Philistine, that he should defy the armies of the
living God?" (1 Samuel 17:26).

Everyone else looked at Goliath and saw a champion; David looked at Goliath and saw an "uncircumcised Philistine."
David, what kind of glasses do you have on?

To that question David might reply, "Everything changed for me the day Samuel anointed me. When I look at my enemies now, under this anointing, I see them in a totally different light. I am no longer intimidated or fearful in the presence of my enemies. And it's all because of that anointing that came upon me from Samuel."

Everyone else looked at Israel's army and saw an incompetent bunch of under-staffed, under-equipped, under-qualified losers. When Saul looked at his army, he got depressed. When the army looked at themselves, they got depressed. But when David looked at them, he saw "the armies of the living God."
David, what kind of glasses do you have on?

"I'm not sure," David might say. "All I know is that ever since the Holy Spirit came upon me at Samuel's anointing, I see the people of God in a totally different light. I no longer see the people of Israel according to the flesh. I see the armies of the living God!"

The anointing transformed how David viewed the enemy and how he viewed the people of God.

David confronted Goliath in that anointing, and it was not long before Goliath was dead and the Philistine army was defeated. After that victory, everyone else was able to see what David had seen all along: Goliath was nothing but an uncircumcised Philistine, and the warriors of Israel were the armies of the living God.

When Samuel anointed David as king, the Holy Spirit came upon David and downloaded to him an uncommon gift of faith. This was the source of David's faith. It was the anointing. The Holy Spirit filled him with the confidence that, just as Goliath was killed by the power of God, the stronghold of Zion would come down by the same means.

If we are to touch David's faith, we must touch his remaining anointing. When the Holy Spirit comes to rest upon us as

He did David, He will grant us the power to believe Him for the stronghold we face.

"Wait a minute," someone might respond. "How do I pursue a kind of anointing that can only be given from heaven?"

Good question. There is a paradox here.

The Paradox of Faith

When we talk about faith, it is not long before we find ourselves bumping into paradox.

Most of the paradoxes of the kingdom surround the topic of faith. That is because God does not want faith to become something that is codified into theological boxes and spiritual formulas. Paradox keeps faith relational and preserves it from becoming formulaic.

One of the paradoxes of faith is this: We are seeking that which can only be given.

Let me explain that statement. Faith is a gift. "It is the gift of God" (Ephesians 2:8). You cannot get faith through willpower or zeal; the only way to get it is by receiving it from God. Either He gives it to you or you don't have it. It is not earned or deserved, but is entirely a free gift.

It is also true, however, that faith is pursued. Twice Paul urged Timothy to "pursue...faith" (1 Timothy 6:11; 2 Timothy 2:22). We know that heaven must give it, but we also pursue it eagerly (in the same way we desire and pursue all of the greatest spiritual gifts, as per 1 Corinthians 12:31). We pursue faith through the reading and hearing of the word (Romans 10:17), through fasting and prayer, through spiritual disciplines, and through intimacy with Jesus.

The paradox makes us ask, "How do I pursue a gift? How can I expect to obtain from God that which cannot be obtained through human effort?"

This paradox will always stay with you as you pursue faith. You will realize you are utterly incapable of apprehending the faith you desire, since only God can give it; but you will also realize that God wants you to pursue this gift with all your soul and strength.

Taking the Kingdom

Paul emphasized that faith must be pursued. Jesus did

not use the word "pursue," He used the word "take." But He meant the same thing. He said we "take" the kingdom by force.

When Jesus talked about taking the kingdom of heaven by force, He meant (among other things) that we should pursue with abandonment the miracles He demonstrated in His ministry. The kingdom of God, according to Jesus, is a place where the blind see and the lame walk. In other words, to take the kingdom of God is tantamount to taking the stronghold of the blind and lame.

> *"The blind see and the lame walk; the lepers are cleansed and the deaf hear; the dead are raised up and the poor have the gospel preached to them...And from the days of John the Baptist until now the kingdom of heaven suffers violence, and the violent take it by force" (Matthew 11:5, 12).*

The stronghold of the blind and lame will be taken only through kingdom violence. That is, by going deep into the Spirit through the word and prayer. To reach into these inner recesses of the heart of the Holy Spirit will require violence and force.

Jesus indicated in the above passage that even He exercised this kind of kingdom violence. Jesus did not just passively accept whatever fell into His lap. He wrestled and took by force the kingdom of heaven and pulled it into earthly realities.

But now we come to another paradox—the paradox between taking and receiving. We know that some things in the kingdom are *taken* (Matthew 11:12); at the same time, some things in the kingdom are *received* (Mark 10:15). The kingdom is both received and taken. Receiving is passive; taking is aggressive. The tension lies in wondering how we can be both passive and aggressive at the same time. How can we know, when we look at the stronghold before us, whether we should be in taking mode or receiving mode?

This is another one of the paradoxes of faith that never totally resolves. God holds us in the tension between receiving and taking because He wants us leaning on Him in dependence and trust. He wants the walk of faith to be *relational*.

Bill Johnson once framed the tension like this: Most of what you need will come to you; most of what you want you will have to go get.

Do your utmost to receive the kingdom. And if you feel like your receiver is not working so good, then use your taker. Use whatever means you must—just get the kingdom!

We're Not Looking Back

As already stated, I am presently a captive in a stronghold of infirmity. Here is one of the Scriptures that has helped my pursuit.

> *Brethren, I do not count myself to have apprehended; but one thing I do, forgetting those things which are behind and reaching forward to those things which are ahead, I press toward the goal for the prize of the upward call of God in Christ Jesus (Philippians 3:13-14).*

Paul's emphasis in this passage is on pressing forward. Paul spoke of "forgetting those things which are behind," and here is one way I personally must do that. I must put behind me the nagging reminder that I have been seeking to overcome this stronghold for eighteen years. It is so tempting to keep reminding myself of that number eighteen. But I am resolved that I will not focus on what I have not been able to attain in years past. I will not become distracted with how long I have been in the fight. Rather, I am going to arise each day with an attitude of, "Today is the day of salvation. This is the day the Lord has made. I am going to pursue faith and this stronghold *today*." This is how I "press toward the goal for the prize of the upward call of God in Christ Jesus."

When I look forward, I find grace to press toward the upward calling.

Using Faith Over and Over

The stronghold before us is a great trial, but one of God's purposes in this trial is to build within us a re-usable kind of faith. God wants us to gain a faith that is so substantial it can be used over and over against similar strongholds.

Paul demonstrated this kind of repeatable faith.

> *And it happened that the father of Publius lay sick of a fever and dysentery. Paul went in to him and prayed, and he laid*

his hands on him and healed him (Acts 28:8)

Paul was used of the Lord to perform many miracles throughout his ministry. Like Joab, he had ascended a water shaft and had procured some spiritual authority against strongholds. However, when faced with the challenge of releasing the father of Publius from a stronghold of sickness, Paul did not take it on casually or presumptuously.

Instead of moving ahead hastily, he went to prayer. "Paul went in to him and prayed." Paul began with prayer because he wanted to recapture the same kind of miracle-working faith he had known in the past. So he began to reach inside in prayer. He was reaching into the places in the Spirit where he had been in the past, seeking to find the substance of faith that he had procured for past victories. He had to go inside to open this stronghold. Paul went deep internally in prayer until he was able to lay hold of the faith he knew he needed. Then, once he had that kind of faith in his grip, he laid his hands upon Publius's father and healed him.

Paul was showing us that once you have touched certain realms of faith, there is a way through prayer to visit those realms of faith again and release other prisoners from their strongholds.

Peter demonstrated the same thing. Peter was used powerfully of the Lord in releasing many captives from strongholds of infirmity. Then, when he was faced with the challenge of raising Dorcas from the stronghold of death, he did the same thing that Paul did with Publius's father. Let me back up and tell the story.

Dorcas was a believer in Joppa who had died. Upon her death, the disciples called for Peter to come from nearby Lydda to pray over her corpse. They brought Peter to the room where her body lay.

> *But Peter put them all out, and knelt down and prayed. And turning to the body he said, "Tabitha, arise." And she opened her eyes, and when she saw Peter she sat up (Acts 9:40).*

What was the first thing Peter did? "Peter put them all out, and knelt down and prayed." Why did Peter start with prayer? Because he was doing the same thing Paul did with Publius's father. He was reaching down, in the Spirit, to access the kind of faith he had found many times previously. He knew the doors of death would be opened from the inside. So he went inside, reaching for faith. Once he had a grip on faith for the stronghold before him, he turned to the body and raised Dorcas up.

Both Paul and Peter were drawing, in prayer, upon their past experience in God. In the same way, God wants to give you your own history in faith so that, once your first stronghold is taken, you can use that same quality of faith again and again to bring down other strongholds.

Rees Howells and Hitler

My favorite story from Rees Howells demonstrates this same principle.

Rees was a man whom God had schooled in the privileges and power of intercession. His intercessory ministry came to its zenith during World War II. God used Rees and his band of prayer warriors to achieve spiritual victories ahead of physical victories in the war. They learned to bring strongholds down in the Spirit realm and once the victory was gained in the Spirit, it would be followed soon after by actual military victories over the Nazi army.

My favorite of all Rees's stories regards the time that Hitler's armies were advancing on Egypt. To all appearances, nothing would be able to stop the Nazi onslaught. If Egypt were to fall, the Nazi army would steamroller over Palestine and the Bible lands. But the Lord had revealed to Rees His plan to return the Jews to their homeland of Palestine, so that the gospel might go out to every creature and Christ return to earth. Hitler, therefore, must not be allowed to conquer Palestine. He must be stopped before he takes Alexandria, Egypt. Unto this end, Rees Howells and his community of praying friends went into intercession.

Rees went deep. He went inside, into the recesses of the Spirit that he had learned to navigate, and he began to take on the stronghold of the Nazi army in North Africa.

When Rees had finally prayed his way through to faith, he describes his attainment of faith through intercession in the most remarkable language.

I thought he might be allowed to take Egypt, but now I know he [Hitler] will never take Egypt—neither Alexandria nor Cairo will fall...I have been stirred to my depths today. I have been like a man ploughing his way through sand. But now I am on top of it; now I am gripping it. I am handling it; I can shake it. [1]

I love the way Rees articulated his attainment of faith. He went inside to get it. When he finally laid hold of faith in the Holy Spirit for Egypt, that faith was so tangible to him that it seemed as real as something his fingers could grip. The hands of his spirit were totally wrapped around the assurance of divine intervention. He knew that God would deliver Egypt from the Nazi war machine.

And sure enough, Rommel and his armored divisions never took Egypt. His armies were thwarted at the border of Egypt, in the battle of El Alamein, in a most peculiar and unanticipated manner.[2] It was an answer from heaven. Rees had found a faith in God that he could use over and again.

The Keys of the Kingdom

Faith is like a key. When God gives you faith for a stronghold, it's like He's handing you a key. When you turn that key, the gate to that stronghold swings open easily.

Here is how Jesus spoke of it.

"And I will give you the keys of the kingdom of heaven, and whatever you bind on earth will be bound in heaven, and whatever you loose on earth will be loosed in heaven" (Matthew 16:19).

---

1   The entire story is worth reading. You'll find it in: Norman Grubb, *Rees Howells, Intercessor*; CLC Publications, Fort Washington, PA, 2001, p. 251.

2   One deciding incident in the battle of El Alamein regards a water pipe. The Germans, dehydrated from lack of water, came across a water pipe, shot holes into it, and drank deeply of the water. Their senses were too parched to realize that the pipe contained salt water. Consequently, with hands above their heads, 1,100 of Germany's elite troops stumbled in surrender toward the British lines at Alexandria, their swollen, bloody-black tongues protruding from their mouths. Crazily they tore water bottles from the necks of British soldiers in order to sooth their parched lips.

When you face a formidable stronghold, one of the prayers you will probably find yourself praying is, "Lord, give me the key to this stronghold." Each stronghold requires its own key. When Jesus gives you the key to a stronghold, kingdom doors open and captives are loosed. "'Whatever you loose on earth will be loosed in heaven.'"

Strongholds are not opened by trying out every key you know to use. "That key didn't work—here, let's try this one." No, you will not open the stronghold by trying first this method, then that.

To open the stronghold, Jesus must give you the specific key. Until He gives it, all you can do is go deep, go inside, and seek Him for the key.

Here is the glory of Christ's words: "'I *will* give you the keys of the kingdom of heaven.'" Jesus has made it a bold promise—He *will* give us keys to the strongholds we face.

I am writing this to encourage your faith. Go deep. Ask for the keys. He will give them to you.

Glorify Your Son

I want to encourage your faith with one final Scripture. I love to pray from this Scripture, from the words Jesus prayed to His Father at the end of His earthly ministry.

> *Jesus spoke these words, lifted up His eyes to heaven, and said: "Father, the hour has come. Glorify Your Son, that Your Son also may glorify You" (John 17:1).*

Jesus had in view the stronghold He was about to enter— hell itself. He was about to die on the cross and descend into the stronghold of Sheol, the place of the departed. He recognized that the hour of His departure had come.

His request of His Father, therefore, was this: "Glorify Your Son, that Your Son also may glorify You." Jesus was saying, "Abba, I'm asking You to raise Me up from the stronghold of death and the grave. Glorify Me. Raise Me up to glory. Open the gates of hell, lift Me up, and glorify Me once again at Your right hand." Then Jesus went on to make a covenant with His Father. "Abba, if You will glorify Me by lifting Me out of the stronghold of death, I promise that I will glorify You. I will magnify Your name in every nation on earth. I will glorify You before the entire human race. This is My promise, Abba. If you will glorify Me, I will glorify You."

I have made the same promise in prayer to the Father. I have said, "Abba, glorify me and I will glorify You. Lift me out of this pit, release me from the captivity of this stronghold and glorify me with a testimony of Your grace, and I promise to use all the strength of my soul to glorify You in the earth."

Make this your prayer of faith. "Lift me up out of this stronghold, Abba, and I will lift You up. Raise me up and I'll raise You up. Glorify Your son that Your son may glorify You."

13

Invitation to All

Now David said on that day, "Whoever climbs up by way
of the water shaft and defeats the Jebusites...he shall be
chief and captain" (2 Samuel 5:8).

Joab was the one who climbed up the water shaft and led the
defeat of the Jebusites. However, he had not been appointed
or hand-selected by David in advance for that task. David did
not say to him, "Joab, you have a divine mandate on your life
to take the stronghold of Zion. I have chosen you for this job. I
believe you're the man for it."

No, David did not approach Joab at all. Instead, he issued
a general invitation to the entire nation. The announcement was
proclaimed throughout the land, "Whoever climbs up the water
shaft and defeats the Jebusites will be captain of the army."

The word I am highlighting in David's invitation is the
word, "Whoever." The challenge to penetrate the stronghold
was given equally to every warrior in the nation. It was an invitation to all.

The same invitation is going forth today by the Holy Spirit—
to "whoever." There is a stronghold of infirmity in the church,
and the Holy Spirit is issuing a universal invitation to all believers. Whoever is willing, let him climb up by way of the water
shaft and open the stronghold of infirmity from the inside.

Do not think you must be sovereignly called and appointed
of God to this task. You must simply be willing and motivated
enough to take it on.

Has God given you enough incentive to take on the stronghold before you? Are you willing to fight for the inheritance of

the church in your region? Do you desire to hasten the coming of the Lord? Do you see the implications for both this age and the age to come? Then "whoever" means you are a candidate. When you take the stronghold of infirmity in your region, that exploit will qualify you for even more abandoned servanthood in the kingdom. Why not lay everything down and go for it?

Get ready to brave the loneliness of the quest. Be prepared to navigate unforeseen darkness. Recognize that the risk of drowning is real. The greatness of the quest makes the risk of the venture seem reasonable.

Go deep in God. Get trained and equipped. Devote yourself to the word, to fasting, and to prayer. Develop an inner life in God. Get absolutely immersed in the Holy Spirit. Pursue a remaining anointing. Listen for divine strategies. Ask for a kingdom key. Get a grip on re-usable faith. Allow the desperation that God has birthed in your spirit to propel you toward the most daring quest of your life. Enter into the bravery of Joab.

Prophesy to those walls that stand before you—high, erect, and looming—and declare in the bold confidence of the Holy Spirit, "You're coming down!"

Our King, the Lord Jesus Christ, is going to take the stronghold of infirmity in the church in this final hour!

Cancer, you are coming down! Multiple sclerosis, you are coming down! Schizophrenia, you are coming down! Diabetes, you must surrender! AIDS, you cannot resist our Champion. To the blind we say, you shall see! The deaf shall hear! The mute shall speak! To the paralytics we declare, you shall leap for joy!

> *Then the eyes of the blind shall be opened, and the ears of the deaf shall be unstopped. Then the lame shall leap like a deer, and the tongue of the dumb sing (Isaiah 35:5-6).*

Then the Lord Jesus will come and establish His throne in Zion. Even so, come, Lord Jesus!

Appendix

Why Zion was Important

Beautiful in elevation, the joy of the whole earth, is Mount Zion on the sides of the north, the city of the great King (Psalm 48:2).

When David set his sights on Jerusalem, he was tapping into a spiritual stream of prophetic significance that was centuries old. Jerusalem had been on God's mind for a long time. It's a city whose profound spiritual history reached back a thousand years before David to the time of Abraham.

The first mention of Jerusalem[1] in the Bible occurs in Genesis 14, at a time when Lot had been carried captive by invading forces. In a stunning military victory, Abraham delivered Lot from his captors and brought him safely home. Upon his return, Melchizedek went out to meet Abraham and bless him. Melchizedek was the king of Jerusalem (Salem) and also the priest of God Most High (see Genesis 14:14-24). Since Zion was Jerusalem's safest neighborhood and thus its most ancient neighborhood—the "old city" if you will—it is reasonable to conclude that Melchizedek's throne was in Zion proper (even though it wasn't called Zion at the time). We could say, therefore, that Melchizedek came out of Zion in order to bless Abraham.

There was a second time when Abraham quietly brushed with Zion—when Abraham led his son, Isaac, to Mount Moriah,

---

1   Jerusalem's most ancient name was Salem, Genesis 14:18. Later it was called Jebus, Joshua 18:28. Later still, the two names were joined to form the contemporary name, Jerusalem.

bound him, and placed him on a makeshift altar (see Genesis 22). Abraham intended to obey God's voice and sacrifice his only son. A voice from heaven stopped him, and instead God provided a ram for the burnt offering. This all happened on Moriah.

Moriah is a hill within the city limits of contemporary Jerusalem. Moriah was the place where Solomon built his temple, and today it is the site of the Mosque of Omar (the Dome of the Rock). So when Abraham was on Moriah, he would have been within eyeshot of Zion and Melchizedek's governmental seat. There is no biblical hint that he popped in on Melchizedek at that time, but the proximity would have made it very easy to do.

Melchizedek was the first priest of God to appear in Scripture, and it was no coincidence that his throne was in Zion (called Salem at the time). Jesus Christ was later declared to be a Priest in the order of Melchizedek (Psalm 110:4). As such, Jesus is the rightful heir to the throne of Zion.

The Bible draws a great line of prophetic purpose between Melchizedek and Jesus Christ (see Hebrews 5-7). David stepped into the matrix of that divine purpose when he chose, under Holy Spirit direction, to conquer Zion.

And like Melchizedek before him, David was called of God to function in both a kingly and priestly capacity. This is why we see David putting on a linen ephod—which was a garment for priests to wear—at the procession of the ark to Zion (1 Chronicles 15:27). As a king, David was claiming also to be a priest. We know, however, that David was not pretending to be a Levitical priest since he was not of the tribe of Levi. Of what priesthood was he, then? There is only one remaining possibility. Clearly, David saw himself serving the Lord as a priest in the order of Melchizedek—a priesthood that is both priestly and kingly. David had no right to serve as a priest in the Aaronic order, but as a priest in the order of Melchizedek he was given divine permission to place the ark in open view, sit before it, and minister to the Lord.

While serving in this priestly capacity, David was shown that Messiah would serve before God in the same priesthood. This is why David wrote, "The LORD has sworn and will not relent, 'You are a priest forever according to the order of Melchizedek'" (Psalm 110:4). David's zeal for Zion was rooted in his understanding that one day Messiah would rule in Jerusalem as a Priest/King, just like Melchizedek did centuries before.

Jerusalem is a city like none other! It holds the distinction of being the only place on earth God chose as His eternal home (see Psalm 132:13-14). This is why history revolves around this city and God's agenda for it. There are said to be 685 cities in the earth with a population larger than Jerusalem, and yet Jerusalem makes international headlines consistently more than most of them. What is the deal with Jerusalem, anyway? Why is it the most important city on earth? What makes it so different from other cities?

The answer is that God's eyes and interests are riveted upon Jerusalem and, consequently, so are Satan's. No location on earth matches Jerusalem for intensity of heavenly attention and spiritual warfare.

Zion and Jerusalem

The name Zion was used initially in Scripture for the small citadel inside Jerusalem where David placed his throne. Over time, however, the Holy Spirit began to broaden the concept of Zion in Scripture until it sometimes referred to all of Jerusalem (e.g., Psalm 76:2), or even the entire nation of Israel (e.g., Isaiah 3:16). When Zion is mentioned in the Bible, therefore, the precise meaning of the term can vary a bit depending on the context.

I find the following definition helpful. *Zion is Jerusalem, particularly in regard to her Davidic inheritance.* By "her Davidic inheritance," I mean the promise of God to establish the Son of David upon the throne of Zion forever (Psalm 89:3-4, 29, 35-37; 132:11-18).

God had this to say about Zion: "For Zion's sake I will not hold My peace, and for Jerusalem's sake I will not rest, until her righteousness goes forth as brightness, and her salvation as a lamp that burns" (Isaiah 62:1). No wonder Jerusalem is in the news almost every day! God Himself is resolved to labor without rest until Jerusalem's righteousness and salvation shines brightly in the earth.

Jerusalem's salvation is not even remotely seen right now. Men look at her today and see reproach, strife, stubbornness, and religious wars. What will it take to transform Jerusalem from its current condition to a city that shines brightly before the whole earth? Only one thing can effect that kind of transformation—the physical return of Jesus Christ. Only when Jesus establishes His throne in Zion will Jerusalem become a praise in all the earth (see Isaiah 62:7).

Zion: Political and Worship Capital

God chose the most impenetrable fortress in the entire land of Canaan as the geographical seat of Christ's throne and authority. Zion's reputation as unconquerable reflected the enduring nature of Christ's Kingdom. "His kingdom is the one which shall not be destroyed, and His dominion shall endure to the end" (Daniel 6:26).

David established his throne in Zion as a prophetic declaration that eventually his Son, the Messiah, would reign in that exact place. In David's time, Zion's primary identity was the governmental seat for David's throne. Using an American term, Zion was David's "White House."

Once he established his political capital in Zion, David then used his authority to establish Zion as a seat for 24/7 worship to the Lord (1 Chronicles 25). David understood the pattern of worship in the heavenlies (Psalm 119:96). He observed that wherever God's throne is established there is incessant worship arising before Him. To fulfill that divine pattern, David inaugurated 24/7 worship and prayer in the stronghold of Zion. That 24/7 house of prayer represented the worship and praise that will arise incessantly to Jesus when He returns to earth and places His throne in Zion. Davidic-style worship will continue in Zion forever.

Zion, therefore, represents two things. Zion is:

- The seat of governmental authority, and
- The seat of incessant worship.

When David conquered Zion, it was so that he might establish both realities in Zion in their proper order.

We are watching an unprecedented phenomenon taking place in the earth right now. 24/7 houses of prayer are arising throughout the earth. As incessant worship is established before the Lord of God, it provides an atmosphere where the governmental authority of Christ in the earth can be exercised. And the inverse is also true: Whenever the kingdom of God is established with authority in a region, it makes a way for 24/7 houses of prayer to be raised up in that region.

David's First Order of Business

David was promised by Samuel that he would be king of Israel, but it did not happen all at once. First he went through approximately ten years of refining in the wilderness. The latter part of that season was spent in exile in the land of the Philistines. Once his preparation was complete, he was given the kingdom of Israel in two stages.

In the first stage, David was crowned king only of the tribe of Judah. Being of the tribe of Judah himself, his relatives were first to crown him. He reigned over Judah for seven years from the capital city of Hebron, while Ishbosheth, Saul's son, reigned over the other eleven tribes. During this time Jerusalem lay within the boundaries of the tribe of Benjamin and was, therefore, outside David's jurisdiction.

Seven years later Ishbosheth died. Then the eleven tribes of Israel gathered together and asked David to reign over all twelve tribes of Israel. For the next thirty-three years, David was king over the entire nation.

Once David was crowned king of the twelve tribes, Jerusalem came under his jurisdiction. David had been waiting for this moment and immediately sprang to action regarding Zion.

As you read the biblical passages below, notice how one event followed the other. First came David's coronation as king.

> *Then all the tribes of Israel came to David at Hebron and spoke, saying, "Indeed we are your bone and your flesh. Also, in time past, when Saul was king over us, you were the one who led Israel out and brought them in; and the LORD said to you, 'You shall shepherd My people Israel, and be ruler over Israel.'" Therefore all the elders of Israel came to the king at Hebron, and King David made a covenant with them at Hebron before the LORD. And they anointed David king over Israel. David was thirty years old when he began to reign, and he reigned forty years. In Hebron he reigned*

over Judah seven years and six months, and in Jerusa-
lem he reigned thirty-three years over all Israel and Judah
(2 Samuel 5:1-5).

I want you to notice, now, the next verse in the Bible. What
was David's very first act as king of Israel? Look at it.

And the king and his men went to Jerusalem against the
Jebusites, the inhabitants of the land, who spoke to David,
saying, "You shall not come in here; but the blind and the
lame will repel you," thinking, "David cannot come in here."
*Nevertheless David took the stronghold of Zion (that **is**, the*
City of David) (2 Samuel 5:6-7).

First came the coronation over the twelve tribes; then came
the conquest of Zion. David's very first order of business as
king of the entire land was to target the stronghold of Zion.
Clearly, Zion was in his crosshairs all along, but he could not
engage the stronghold as long as it lay outside his political jurisdiction. Once he had the authority to do something about it,
he did not pause for the slightest moment but headed straight
for Zion.